S0-AYG-851

GOTTHOLD EPHRAIM LESSING

NATHAN THE WISE

A Dramatic Poem in Five Acts

Translated into English Verse by
Bayard Quincy Morgan

A Frederick Ungar Book
CONTINUUM • NEW YORK

KVCC KALAMAZOO VALLEY
COMMUNITY COLLEGE
LIBRARY

JAN 1 6 2008

1988

The Continuum Publishing Company
370 Lexington Avenue
New York, NY 10017

Twelfth Printing

Copyright © 1955, 1983 by Frederick Ungar Publishing Co.

All rights reserved. No part of this book may be reproduced,
stored in a retrieval system, or transmitted, in any form or
by any means, electronic, mechanical, photocopying, recording,
or otherwise, without the written permission of
The Continuum Publishing Company.

Printed in the United States of America

Library of Congress Catalog Card Number: 55-8745

ISBN 0-8044-6401-4

INTRODUCTION

LESSING'S POETIC DRAMA, *Nathan the Wise*, is one of the most admirable documents of eighteenth-century thought; it is at the same time — as Goethe's *Faust* is in an even greater degree — both a conclusion and a summing up of its author's productive life. For Lessing had shown as early as 1749, when he was only twenty, his interest in one of the main themes of the drama by writing *Die Juden*, a defense of the Jews against the religious bigotry which was rampant in that day, and the idea of religious tolerance was prominent in his thinking and writing throughout his entire career. However, *Nathan der Weise* was not, like *Faust*, the result of a long-standing plan: it was produced in response to a particular situation and conflict.

Involved in a bitter theological dispute with Chief Pastor Goeze of Hamburg (some of whose unlovely characteristics are assigned to the Patriarch of Jerusalem in this play), Lessing had got much the better of the argument, by virtue of his keen intellect and his rapier-like wit, when Goeze resorted to force and induced the Consistory of Saxony to interdict both the sale and the perusal of Lessing's writings; whereupon the authorities of Brunswick forbade him to publish anything relating to religion without the express permission of the government. Nothing daunted,

Lessing resolved to employ the stage as pulpit, and to preach the doctrine of religious tolerance in such a way as to confute the bigots and the zealots for good and all.

Plot and Sources. In a letter to his brother Karl, Lessing himself revealed the germinal episode around which he built his dramatic action: it was the ancient fable of the three rings, as related in Boccaccio's *Decameron*, the third story of the first day. The reference to Saladin in this version of the tale (which was current in the Middle Ages in a variety of forms) led to the choice of Jerusalem as the stage of action, with the probable date of 1193 as the time, since Saladin died in March of that year and the truce with Richard I had been concluded in September 1192.

Nothing in the drama is more characteristic of Lessing, nothing bears more authentically the stamp of his great heart and soul, than his significant improvement on the Ring-Fable as he has it told to Saladin by Nathan (Act III, Scene 7). It is to be noted in this connection that most supposedly magic objects operate either by means of some intrinsic force or quality (like the seven-league boots, which merely have to be donned) or in response to an appropriate act of the possessor (as when Aladdin rubs the magic lamp). Lessing, however, invents a new category, and raises the whole conception of such an object to a higher plane, when he makes the power of the ring derive from the implicit faith of its wearer:

And had the magic power that he who wore it,
Trusting its strength, was loved of God and man.

And to make sure that this noble conception is driven home, he first has the judge, to whom the irate sons have taken their dispute, point out that

>   The rings' effect is only backward,
>   Not outward . . .

and then convert this negative appraisal into the positive appeal,

>   Then let each one believe his ring to be
>   The true one . . .
>   Let each aspire . . .
>   To match the rest in bringing to the fore
>   The magic of the opal in his ring!

The Characters. The name Nathan (instead of Melchizedek, as in Boccaccio's tale) probably derives from another story in the *Decameron*, while a number of his fine characteristics can be traced to Lessing's friend Moses Mendelssohn. Though he stands for the Jewish race in its finest aspects, Nathan is more freethinker than Jew, and may be regarded as Lessing's own mouthpiece; in the original preface to the work we find the significant statement: "Nathan's attitude toward all positive religion has always been my own."

Counter-figures to Nathan are Saladin the Mussulman and his sister Sittah, who yield little if at all to Nathan in nobility of character. Lessing draws effectively on the historic record involving Saladin; for Sittah, of whom nothing but the name is known, he is thought to have made use of features belonging to Elise Reimarus, the daughter of the scholar whose unorthodox MS Lessing had published, thus eliciting the wrath of Goeze and the faithful generally. The Christians, it must be admitted, seem to come off rather poorly: the Patriarch of Jerusalem is a veritable scoundrel (though not as evil as the historic one), the zealous Daya is a stupid fanatic, and the young Templar, though he shows promise of growth, is still rather unstable and unbalanced. But we must not forget the Lay Brother, Friar Bonafides, who though given a subordinate role incorporates the true spirit of Christianity and is an altogether notable invention.

Nathan's daughter Rachel is thought to bear some resemblance to Lessing's stepdaughter, Amalia König. Some critics find it hard to reconcile her high intellectuality with her credulous belief, no doubt inspired by Daya, that her rescuer was not a man but an angel. Otherwise she rings true throughout, and is most touching in her devotion to Nathan, whose character is thus seen from the side, as it were, in consonance with what we know of him in his full-face aspect.

Finally, there is the Dervish Al-Hafi, one of Lessing's most original creations, to be laughed at and laughed with at the same time.

It is a small cast, remarkably well balanced and used with singular economy.

The Form. In the history of German poetry, *Nathan der Weise* occupies a key position. Up to this time, the French alexandrine (iambic hexameter) had been the preferred form of dramatic verse. Lessing had felt the power of Shakespeare, and in this drama he adapted blank verse to his own language. When Goethe, in his revision of *Iphigenie auf Tauris,* followed Lessing's lead, the victory of blank verse in German drama was assured.

Nathan on the Stage. Contrary to Lessing's own expectations, *Nathan der Weise* became a notable stage success, and the role of Nathan has been regarded as one of the great vehicles for significant acting. Under the Nazis, of course, the drama was banned; but after the war it had for a time more performances than any other play, and today it is in the standard repertory of all the larger theatres.

B. Q. M.

BIBLIOGRAPHY

(Most of the important works on Lessing are in German, but all major encyclopedias contain articles on him, and histories of German literature deal extensively with him.)

Lowell, James Russell. *Among My Books*. Boston, 1879; also, Lowell's *Writings*, Vol. II. Boston, 1897.

Rolleston, T. W. *Life of G. E. Lessing*. London, 1889.

Sime, James. *Lessing*. 2d ed., London, 1879.

Stahr, Adolf. *G. E. Lessing*, tr. E. P. Evans. Boston, 1866.

(There are several textbook editions of *Nathan der Weise;* each has a good introduction and numerous notes, some of which contribute to the interpretation of the play.)

PRINCIPAL DATES OF LESSING'S LIFE

1729   Born at Kamenz (Lusatia).

1747   Entered the University of Leipzig; *Damon oder die wahre Freundschaft* (play).

1748   Berlin; Plays: *Der junge Gelehrte; Der Misogyn.*

1749   Plays: *Die Juden; Der Freigeist.*

1752   M. A. Wittenberg.

1753–55   Collected *Works*, 6 vols.

1755   *Miss Sara Sampson* (prose drama).

1759   *Philotas* (tragedy).

1759–65   *Briefe die neuste Literatur betreffend* (essays).

1760   Secretary to General Tauentzien in Breslau.

1766   *Laokoon oder über die Grenzen der Malerei und der Poesie* (esthetic theory).

1767   *Minna von Barnhelm* (comedy).

1767–69   *Hamburgische Dramaturgie* (critical essays).

1770–81   Wolfenbüttel, (ducal) librarian.

1772   *Emilia Galotti* (tragedy).

1776   Marriage with Eva König.

1778   Death of Eva.

1779   *Nathan der Weise* (drama, blank verse).

1780   *Die Erziehung des Menschengeschlechts* (philosophy).

1781   Death of Lessing.

MOTTO:

Introite, nam et hic Dei sunt! *

APUD GELLIUM

* *Enter, for here too there are gods!*

PERSONS

Sultan SALADIN [1]

SITTAH, his sister

NATHAN, a rich Jew in Jerusalem

RACHEL, his adopted daughter

DAYA, a Christian, but in the house of the Jew, as companion to his daughter

A young Templar [2]

A Dervish [3]

The Patriarch of Jerusalem [4]

A Lay Brother [5]

An Emir [6] and several Mamelukes [7] of Saladin

The scene is Jerusalem.

---

[1] SALADIN (1138–93), sultan of Egypt from 1175, took and entered Jerusalem in 1187. His generosity, gentleness, honesty, and kindness are matters of historic record.

[2] The Knights Templar were members of a religious and military order founded in Jerusalem about 1118; originally they took vows of chastity and poverty. The order was disbanded in 1312.

[3] Dervish is a member of one of the Moslem fraternities; members took vows of poverty.

[4] *Here*, bishop.

[5] Lay brothers and sisters had manual or domestic work assigned to them. This man is FRIAR BONAFIDES (see p. 100).

[6] *Here*, a military commander or general.

[7] *Here*, slaves constituting Saladin's bodyguard.

ACT I

SCENE 1

(Vestibule in Nathan's house.—Nathan returning from a journey. Daya comes to meet him.)

DAYA. It's he, it's Nathan!—Endless thanks to God,
    That you at last return to us again.
NATHAN. Yes, Daya; thanks to God! But why 'at last'?
    Had I intended sooner to return?
    And had I power to do so? Babylon
    Is from Jerusalem two hundred leagues
    By such a road as I perforce must follow,
    With side trips taken to both right and left;
    Collecting debts, you know, is certainly
    No business that proceeds apace, for which   10
    One needs but turn his hand.
DAYA.   O Nathan, Nathan,
    How wretched, wretched meanwhile you might well
    Have come to be at home! Your house . . .
NATHAN.   Took fire.
    So much I have already learned.—God grant
    That there's no evil I have yet to learn!
DAYA. And might have burned completely to the
    ground.
NATHAN. Then, Daya, we'd have built a new one here,
    A more convenient one.
DAYA.   That's true enough!—
    But Rachel by a mere hair's breadth escaped

1

From burning with it.   20
NATHAN.   Burned? My Rachel? she?—
  I was not told of *that*.—Why then! I'd have
  No further need of houses.—Rachel burned
  But for a hair's breadth!—Ah! No doubt she is!
  Is burned in very truth!—Come, out with it!
  Speak out now!—Slay me, torture me no more.—
  I know she's burned to death.
DAYA.   No, if she were,
  Would *my* lips be the ones to tell you so?
NATHAN. Why then affright me so?—O Rachel,
  Rachel!
  My Rachel!
DAYA.   Yours? You call this Rachel yours?
NATHAN. If ever I must needs again forgo   30
  To call this child my child!
DAYA.   And do you call
  All you possess with equal right your own?
NATHAN. Naught with a greater right! For see, all else
  That I possess, good fortune linked with nature
  Bestowed on me. This property alone
  I owe to virtue.
DAYA.   O, how dear you make
  Me pay for all your noble goodness, Nathan!
  If goodness, exercised with such intent,
  Can still be 'goodness' called.
NATHAN.   With such intent?
  You mean . . . ?   40
DAYA.   My conscience . . .
NATHAN.   Listen, Daya, let
  Me tell you first of all . . .
DAYA.   I say, my conscience . . .
NATHAN. What handsome stuff I bought in Babylon.

So rich, and yet so tasteful! I have brought
No finer cloth, not even for my child.
DAYA. Quite useless! For my conscience, I must say,
Will let itself no longer be benumbed.
NATHAN. And how the rings, the pendants for your
ears,
How brooch and necklace will appeal to you,
Which I selected for you in Damascus:
That I would like to see.   50
DAYA.   That's just like you!
If you can only give, and give, and give!
NATHAN. Take just as gladly as I give—and hush!
DAYA. And hush!—Who questions, Nathan, but that
you
Are honesty, great-heartedness itself?
And yet . . .
NATHAN.   And yet a Jew.—Not so,
That's what you'd say?
DAYA.   What I would like to say,
You know quite well.
NATHAN.   Then hush!
DAYA.   I hold my tongue.
Whatever wrong 'fore God results from this,
And I cannot prevent, and cannot change,—
Can *not*—be on your head!   60
NATHAN.   Be on my head!—
But now where is she? where in hiding?—Daya,
If you're deceiving me!—Say, does she know
That I have come?
DAYA.   Why, this I ask of *you*.
The fright still quivers through her every nerve,
And fire is painted by her phantasy
In every scene it paints. In sleep awakes,

In waking sleeps her mind: hence now she's less
Than beast, now more than angel.

NATHAN.   Poor, poor child!
What are we human beings!

DAYA.   Long she lay
This morning with her eyelids closed, and was   70
As dead. Then starting up, she cried, "Hark, hark!
I hear the camels of my father nearing!
Hark, there's his gentle voice itself!"—But then
Her eye grew dim again, and as her head
Was left without the propping of her arm,
It dropped upon the pillow.—I went through
The gate, and saw you coming, really coming!
What wonder! all her soul in every hour
Was constantly with you—and him.—

NATHAN.   With him?
What 'him' is that?   80

DAYA.   With him who saved her life
From fire.

NATHAN.   Who was it? who?—And where is he?
Who saved my Rachel for me, tell me, who?

DAYA. A youthful Templar, whom, some days before,
They brought here to Jerusalem as captive
And Sultan Saladin had pardoned.

NATHAN.   What?
A Templar, whom the Sultan Saladin
Allowed to live? And by a lesser wonder
Could Rachel not be rescued? God!

DAYA.   Just so.
Had he not bravely risked his life for her,
His new-won life, her own would be no more.   90

NATHAN. Where is he, Daya, this heroic man?—

Where is he? Come and lead me to his feet.
Of course you gave as earnest what I left
Of treasure in your hands? and gave him all?
And promised more? far more?

DAYA.   How could we, Nathan?

NATHAN. Not, not?

DAYA.   He came, and no one knows from
    whence.
He went, and no one knows where to.—Devoid
Of previous knowledge, only by his ear
Directed, spreading out his cloak in front,   99
He boldly pressed through flame and smoke toward
The voice that cried for help. We were assured
That he was lost, when out of smoke and flame
Sudden he faced us there, on sturdy arm
Uplifting her. But cold and all unmoved
By our exulting thanks, he sets his booty
Upon the ground, darts off into the folk—
And fades from sight!

NATHAN.   But not, I hope, for ever.

DAYA. Thereafter for some days we still would see him
    Beneath the palm trees strolling back and forth,
    Which stand about the grave of Him who rose.   110
    I neared him with delight, expressed our thanks,
    Besought, enjoined, conjured—but once again
    To come before the gentle creature who
    Could find no peace or rest, until she had
    Wept out her thanks before his feet.

NATHAN.   And he?

DAYA. In vain! He had no ear for our request;
    And poured such bitter scorn on me besides . . .

NATHAN. Until repelled by that . . .

DAYA.   Quite the reverse!
  I went to meet him every day anew,
  And every day I bore his mockery.   120
  What did I not endure! What more had I
  Not suffered gladly!—But this long time now
  He comes no more to seek the lofty palms
  Which shade our Saviour's grave who rose again;
  And no one knows what has become of him.—
  You are amazed? You muse?
NATHAN.   I'm thinking now
  What impress this must make upon a soul
  Like Rachel's. Think, to see oneself so scorned
  By him whom one is so impelled to prize
  Uncommonly; to be so thrust aside   130
  And yet so much attracted;—on my word,
  There must be long dispute twixt head and heart,
  If hate of men or sadness shall prevail.
  Oft it is neither; and our phantasy,
  Which mingles in the strife, turns us to dreamers,
  In whom the head plays heart, and then again
  The heart must play the head.—A poor exchange!—
  The latter, if I know my Rachel well,
  Is Rachel's case: she dreams.
DAYA.   And yet so gently,
  So amiably!   140
NATHAN.   That's dreaming all the same!
DAYA. Especially one—crotchet, if you will,
  Is dear to her. She thinks her Templar knight
  No earthly man nor born of human kind:
  One of the angels, to whose watch and ward
  Her little heart, from childhood on, was glad
  To think her trusted, from the sheltering cloud
  In which he cloaks himself, in fire as well,

To hover near her, all at once as Templar
Appeared to her.—Please do not smile!—Who
  knows?
Or smile and let her keep this one belief,   150
Which Jew and Christian share with Moslem too;—
A sweet delusion, if it be no more!

NATHAN. Sweet to me too!—Go, worthy Daya, go;
  See what she's doing; I would speak with her.—
  Then I will go to seek that wild, capricious
  Protecting angel. If as yet he wills
  To dwell among us here below; if still
  He practices such graceless chivalry;
  Then I will surely find him, and I'll bring
  Him here.   160

DAYA.   You're undertaking much.

NATHAN.   If sweet
  Delusion then makes way for sweeter truth:—
  Believe me, Daya: to us human folk
  A man is always dearer than an angel,—
  Then you'll not censure me, I hope, not me,
  To find your angel-dreamer fully cured?

DAYA. You are so good, and yet so bad withal!
  I'll go.—But hark, but look!—See, there she
  comes.

SCENE 2

(Enter Rachel.)

RACHEL. Then it is really, wholly you, my father?
  I thought you had but sent your voice ahead.
  Where do you bide? What mountains, deserts,
  streams
  Divide us yet? You're wall to wall with me,

And do not haste your Rachel to embrace?
Poor Rachel, who was burned while you were
    gone!—
Almost was burned! Almost. No, do not shudder.
It is a hideous death, to burn. O, O!
NATHAN. My child! My dear, dear child!
RACHEL.   You had to cross
Euphrates, Tigris, Jordan; and—who knows   10
How many streams there were?—How often I
Trembled for you, before the fire had come
So near to me! For since the fire did come
So near to me, to die in water seems
Like rescue, sweet refreshment.—But you are
Not drowned at all; and I, I too am not
Burned up. How we will now rejoice, and praise,
Praise God! For He, He bore you and your boat
On his *invisible* angels' wings across
The treacherous rivers. Likewise it was He   20
Who showed my angel that he *visibly*
On his white wing should bear me through the
    fire—
NATHAN *(aside)*. White wing! Ah yes, the white and
    forespread cloak
The Templar wore.
RACHEL.   That he all visibly
Should bear me through the fire, which by his wing
Was blown aside.—So I have seen an angel,
My angel, face to face.
NATHAN.   Quite meet for Rachel;
And she would see in him nought fairer, sure,
Than he in her.
RACHEL *(smiling)*. Whom do you flatter, father?
The angel, or yourself?   30

NATHAN.   And were it only
  A man—such as they daily are produced
  By Nature—who this service did for you:
  He must to you be angel. Must and would.
RACHEL. Not *such* an angel; no! a genuine one;
  For surely he was genuine!—Have you
  Yourself not taught me that it's possible
  That there are angels, and that God can do
  Such miracles for those who love Him well?
  I love Him.
NATHAN.   And He loves you too; and does
  For you and others miracles every hour;   40
  Indeed, has done them from eternity
  For all of you.
RACHEL.   I like to hear that.
NATHAN.   What?
  Since it would sound quite natural, unexciting,
  If just a real and living Templar knight
  Had saved your life; would that be any less
  A miracle?—The greatest wonder is
  That to us all the true and genuine wonders
  Can come to be so commonplace, and should.
  Without this universal miracle,
  A thinking man might not have used the word   50
  For that which only children should so call,
  Who, gaping, only see the most uncommon,
  The latest happening.
DAYA.   Come, Nathan, would you
  By suchlike subtleties completely shatter
  Her brain, already sadly overwrought?
NATHAN. Leave me in peace!—Were it for Rachel then
  Not miracle enough, that by a *man*

Her life was saved, who first by no small wonder
Must be preserved himself? Yes, no small wonder!
For who has ever heard that Saladin   60
Had spared a Templar's life? or that
A Templar had desired he should be spared
By him? or hoped it? offered for his freedom
More than the leather belt which bore his sword;
At most his dagger?

RACHEL.   This I find conclusive.—
He was no Templar, father; only seemed it.
If captured Templars never, never come
Save to sure death here in Jerusalem;
If none so freely in this city walks
About: how could at night of his free will   70
A Templar save me?

NATHAN.   See now, how ingenious!
Now, Daya, you speak up. For it was you
Who told me he was sent as captive here.
No doubt you know still more.

DAYA.   Well, yes. Indeed,
That's what they say;—and yet they also say
That Saladin this Templar spared because
Of likeness to a brother he had loved
Especially. But as it's twenty years
Since death removed that brother,—he was called,
I don't know how;—he lived, I don't know
    where:—   80
The matter sounds so hardly—credible,
That I suppose there's simply nothing to it.

NATHAN. Well, Daya! Tell me why that should be so
Incredible. I hope not—such things happen—
Because a thing still more incredible
You'd like to think?—And why should Saladin,

Who dearly loves his kinfolk, one and all,
Not have possessed in younger years a brother
Whom he loved specially?—Do faces not
Resemble one another?—Is an old   90
Impression lost?—Does a like cause no more
Have like effects?—Since when?—What then is here
Incredible?—But that, wise Daya, you
Would think no miracle, and only yours
Requi . . . deserve, I mean to say, belief.

DAYA. You mock.

NATHAN.   Because you're mocking me.—But
    still,
My Rachel, your deliverance even so
Remains a wonder, wrought alone by Him
Who stern resolves, the most ambitious plans
Of kings—His sport if not His mockery—   100
Delights to guide by feeble threads.

RACHEL.   My father!
My father, if I'm wrong, you know it's not
By choice.

NATHAN.   Contrariwise, you like to learn.—
Look here! a forehead, arched this way or that;
The profile of a nose, outlined like this
And not like that; eyebrows which serpentine
On sharp or blunted bone, or so, or so;
A line, a curve, an angle, wrinkle, mole,
A nothing, on a random countenance
From Europe:—and you're saved from fire, in
    Asia!—   110
Is that no wonder, wonder-avid folk?
Why must you call an angel down from Heaven?

DAYA. What harm is there—if I may speak a word—
In spite of all, if one should still prefer

An angel to a man as rescuer?
Does one not feel thereby so much the nearer
To that mysterious First Cause of his rescue?
NATHAN. Nothing but pride! mere pride! The iron pot
    Wants to be drawn with silver tongs from out
    The fire, to think itself a pot of silver.—Bah!— 120
    And what's the harm, you ask me, what's the harm?
    No, what's the good, I'll ask you in return—
    For your "To feel oneself the nearer God"
    Is either nonsense or it's blasphemy.—
    But there is harm; yes, truly, harm indeed.—
    Come, hark to me!—I'm sure, to him who saved
    Your life—and be it angel or a man—
    You both would give, and you, my Rachel, most,
    An ample service in return?—Not so?—
    Well, to an angel, what's the chance that you   130
    Can do him service, ample service, too?
    Thank him you can; can sigh and pray; can melt
    In ecstasy; and on his festal day
    Can fast, give alms.—All futile.—For I think
    In such a case you and your neighbor man
    Will always gain far more than he. He grows
    Not fat from all your fasting; grows not rich
    With your almsgiving; gets no greater glory
    From all your rapture, nor a greater power
    From all your trust. Not so? But if a man!   140
DAYA. It's true we'd have more opportunity,
    Were he a man, to make him some return.
    God knows how ready we were so to do!
    But then, you see, he wanted, needed nothing;
    Was in and with himself so self-contained
    As only angels have the power to be.
RACHEL. And when at last he disappeared . . .

NATHAN.   He did?—
  How disappeared?—He showed himself no more
  Beneath the palms?—Or did you really try
  To see him further?   150
DAYA.   No, indeed we didn't.
NATHAN. No, Daya, no? Now see what harm it does!—
  You cruel dreamers!—Now what if this angel—
  Has fallen sick? . . .
RACHEL.   Sick!
DAYA.   Sick! He won't do that!
RACHEL. What awesome chill assails me! Daya, feel!
My forehead, always warm, is turned to ice.
NATHAN. He is a Frank, not used to such a climate;
  Is young; to tasks demanded by his order,
  To hunger, waking, little used.
RACHEL.   Sick, sick!
DAYA. It's possible, that's all that Nathan means.
NATHAN. Now there he lies, has neither friend
        nor coin   160
  To pay for friendliness.
RACHEL.   O dear, my father!
NATHAN. Lies without tending, comfort, or advice,
  A prey to pain and death!
RACHEL.   Where, where?
NATHAN.   And he,
  Who for a girl he'd never known nor seen—
  Enough that she was human—plunged in fire . . .
DAYA. O spare her, Nathan!
NATHAN.   Who the girl he'd saved
  Would not approach or see again, to save
  Her thanking him . . .
DAYA.   O spare her, Nathan!
NATHAN.   Nor

Desired to see her more—unless it were
That he a second time should save her life,—   170
Being a human soul . . .

DAYA.   O stop, look here!

NATHAN. In dying now he lacks for comfort, all—
Except awareness of his deed.

DAYA.   Stop, stop!
You're killing her!

NATHAN.   And you have murdered him!—
You could have killed him so.—Come, Rachel, Ra-
chel!
It's medicine, not poison, that I give.
He lives!—Recover!—nor is sick, I think;
Not even sick!

RACHEL.   For sure?—not dead? not sick?

NATHAN. For sure, not dead!—For God rewards good
deeds,
Done here, among us.—Go!—But see how far   180
It's easier to swoon in pious dreams
Than do good actions? see how sluggish men
Are fond of dreaming piously, because—
Although at times of their intent not quite
Aware —they'd shun the need of doing good?

RACHEL. O father, never leave me any more
Alone!—But don't you think he might have gone
Upon a journey?

NATHAN.   Silly geese!—Of course.—
I see out there a Mussulman who's eyeing
With curious gaze my camels and their load.   190
I wonder if you know him.

DAYA.   Yes! your dervish.

NATHAN. Who?

DAYA. It's your dervish, and your chess companion.

NATHAN. Al-Hafi? That Al-Hafi?
DAYA.   Treasurer
  Of Saladin.
NATHAN.   Al-Hafi? Are you dreaming?
  It's he!—It's really he!—He's coming here.
  Get in with you, be quick! *(Daya and Rachel leave.)*
    What shall I hear?

SCENE 3

(Enter Al-Hafi richly dressed.)

DERVISH. Open your eyes, as wide as ever you can!
NATHAN. Is it you? Or is it not?—In such attire,
  A dervish! . . .
DERVISH.   Well, why not? Can nought be made
  Out of a dervish, absolutely nothing?
NATHAN. Oh yes, enough!—But I had always thought
  A dervish—if a real one—would allow
  Nought to be made of him.
DERVISH.   Now by the prophet!
  That I'm no real one, that may well be true.
  Yet if one must—
NATHAN.   Must! Dervish!—Dervish must?
  No man needs must, and must a dervish, then?   10
  What must he?
DERVISH.   What one warmly begs of him
  And he admits is good: that must a dervish.
NATHAN. Now, by our God, you speak the truth.—
    Let me
  Embrace you, man.—I hope you're still my friend?
DERVISH. And you don't ask what I have now become?
NATHAN. Despite what you've become!

DERVISH.   Why, could I not
Have come to be a fellow in the State
Whose friendship you'd not want?
NATHAN.   No, if your heart
Is dervish still, I'll risk it. For your office
Of State is but a robe.   20
DERVISH.   Which yet must have
Its honor.—Guess!—What do you think I'd be
If you were king?
NATHAN.   A dervish; and that's all.
But on the side, I fancy, also—cook.
DERVISH. Of course! And thus my trade unlearn?—
A cook!
Not waiter too?—Confess that Saladin
Knows me much better.—I'm his treasurer
At present.
NATHAN.   You?—for him?
DERVISH.   Please understand:
The smaller treasure—for his father wields
The great one still—the treasure for his house.
NATHAN. His house is large.   30
DERVISH.   And larger than you think;
For every beggar-man is of his house.
NATHAN. Yet Saladin so hates the beggar-folk—
DERVISH. That he's resolved to wipe all beggars out
Both root and branch—though he himself thereby
Become a beggar.
NATHAN.   Right!—That's what I mean.
DERVISH. He is one, too, as good as any! For
His treasure is by sunset every day
Much emptier than empty. Be the flood
At morning never so high, by noon long since
It's ebbed away —   40

NATHAN.   Since channels have in part
  Absorbed it which to fill up or to block
  Is equally impossible.
DERVISH.   You've hit it!
NATHAN. I know that game.
DERVISH.   I grant it's not so good
  When princes play the vulture amid corpses.
  But if they're corpses 'mid the vultures, then
  It's ten times worse.
NATHAN.   Not so, my dervish, no!
DERVISH. It's easy, friend, for you to talk.—See here:
  What will you give if I resign my post
  For you?
NATHAN.   What does your post bring in?   50
DERVISH.   To me?
  Not much. But you would make a splendid profit.
  For when the fund's at ebb—as frequently—
  You'll open up your sluices: make advances,
  And take in interest to your heart's desire.
NATHAN. And interest on interest?
DERVISH.   Of course!
NATHAN. Till capital turns into interest.
DERVISH. That doesn't tempt you? Then you'll bid
    farewell
  To this our friendship, now. For I confess
  I counted much on you.
NATHAN.   No, really? What
  Had you in mind?   60
DERVISH.   I hoped that with your help
  My office I'd conduct in honor; that
  I'd always have full credit at your hands.—
  You shake your head?
NATHAN.   Let's try to get this clear!

For one must make distinctions.—You? Why not?
Al-Hafi is as dervish always welcome
To all I have and can.—As treasurer
Of Saladin, Al-Hafi is a man
Who—whom—

DERVISH. I guessed it was so! You are ever
As good as shrewd, as shrewd as you are wise!—
But patience! What in Hafi you distinguish,   70
Shall soon be quite distinct again.—See here
This robe of honor, given by Saladin.
Before it fades and turns to rags, such as
Were fitter far to clothe a dervish, in
Jerusalem you'll see it on a nail,
And I'll be by the Ganges,* walking, barefoot
And lightly clad, the hot sand with my teachers.

NATHAN. That sounds like you.

DERVISH.   And playing chess with them.

NATHAN. Your greatest joy!

DERVISH.   Imagine what seduced me!—
That I myself no longer need go begging?   80
That I might play the rich man among beggars?
That I'd have power to turn the richest beggar
Into a wretched Croesus** in a trice?

NATHAN. I fancy not.

DERVISH.   A thing much more absurd!
For once I felt myself sincerely flattered;
By Saladin's good-hearted error flattered—

NATHAN. Namely?

DERVISH.   He said that only a beggar knows
How beggars feel; that none but a beggar could

---

* The sacred river of northern India.
** The last king of Lydia (560–546 B.C.), whose great wealth
has become proverbial.

Have learned the proper way to give to beggars.
Said he, "Your predecessor was too cold,   90
Too rude for me. He gave ungraciously;
Inquired so savagely of the receiver
Before he gave; he thought it not enough
To know the human need, no, he must learn
The cause of it as well, so that the gift
He'd stingily apportion to that cause.
Al-Hafi won't do that! Nor Saladin
In him appear so stingy-generous!
Al-Hafi is not like to clogged-up pipes,
Which take up crystal-clear and quiet water   100
And spray it out so cloudy and impure.
Al-Hafi thinks, Al-Hafi feels like me!"—
So sweetly sang the fowler's pipe, until
The simpleton was in the net,—I, fool!
Fool of an arrant fool!

NATHAN.   Come, dervish, softly,
   Speak softly!

DERVISH. Stuff!—It were not folly, then,
   A hundred thousand people to oppress,
   Exhaust and plunder, torture, throttle; and
   To single persons play philanthropist?
   It were not foppery, God's ample grace,   110
   Which without choice on good and bad alike,
   On mead and desert, now in rain, now sunshine,
   Is spread abroad, to try to ape, and yet
   To lock the everlasting fullness of His hand?
   It were not foppery. . . .

NATHAN.   Enough, enough!

DERVISH. No, let at least my own unhappy folly
   Be mentioned too!—It were not foppery
   To seek the goodly phases of this nonsense

And take, just for the sake of those good phases,
Your share in all that foppery? Not, not?   120
NATHAN. Al-Hafi, hurry with all speed to get
You back into your desert. For I fear
That being among men you might forget
To be a man.
DERVISH.   You're right, I fear that too.
Farewell! *(Exit Al-Hafi.)*
NATHAN.   So hasty?—Wait, Al-Hafi, wait!
Your desert won't escape you, will it? Wait!
I wish he'd hear me! Hey, Al-Hafi, here!—
He's gone; and I'd have gladly asked of him
Some news about our Templar. Probably   130
He knows of him.

SCENE 4

(Enter Daya in haste.)

DAYA.   O Nathan, Nathan!
NATHAN.   Well?
What now?
DAYA.   He shows himself again! He shows
Himself again!
NATHAN.   Who, Daya, who?
DAYA.   He, he!
NATHAN. He? he?—When doesn't *he* appear? I see,
Your he is the only one.—That should not be!
And were he angel, that would not be right.
DAYA. Again he's strolling up and down beneath
The palms; and plucking dates from time to time.
NATHAN. And eats them?—As a Templar?
DAYA.   Why torment

Me so?—Her greedy eye divined him there   10
Behind the interlacing palms; and now
It follows him. She begs you then—conjures
You rather—go to him without delay.
O haste! She'll signal to you from the window,
Which way he turns, this way or farther off.
O haste!

NATHAN. Dressed as I got down from my camel?—
Would that be proper?—Haste to him yourself,
Report my safe return. This gentleman,
You'll see, was loath to enter my abode
While I was gone; will not refuse to come   20
If I invite as father. Go and say
I beg him cordially . . .

DAYA.   In vain! To you
He will not come.—In brief: he shuns all Jews.

NATHAN. Then go at least to hold him where he is;
At least that you may follow with your eyes
The course he takes.—Go, I will soon be there.

(Nathan hurries inside, Daya outside.)

SCENE 5

(An open space with palms, under which the Templar
is walking up and down. A friar follows him at some
distance and to one side, always as if about to address
him.)

TEMPLAR. He follows not to pass the time.—And look,
See how he eyes my hands—My worthy brother . . .
Or I might call you Father, too, no doubt?

FRIAR. No, brother; just lay brother; at your service.

TEMPLAR. Ah, goodly brother, had I anything!

God knows that I have nothing—

FRIAR.   All the same
Right hearty thanks! God grant a thousandfold
What you would like to give. For it's the will
And not the gift that makes the giver.—And
I was not sent to follow you for alms.   10

TEMPLAR. Yet you were sent?

FRIAR.   Yes, from the monastery.

TEMPLAR. Where I but now a pilgrim meal had hoped
To find?

FRIAR.   The benches were all filled, but yet
You should return with me.

TEMPLAR.   What for? It's true
I've long dispensed with meat; but then, what odds?
The dates are ripe, you know.

FRIAR.   Sir, but beware
Of too much of that fruit: that is not good,
It clogs the spleen, makes melancholy blood.

TEMPLAR. And what if sadness suits me?—Though, I
  think,
Not just to give this warning you were sent?   20

FRIAR. O no!—My mission was to sound you out;
To feel your pulse a bit.

TEMPLAR.   And this you tell
Yourself, like that?

FRIAR.   Why not?

TEMPLAR (aside).   A waggish brother!
  (Aloud.) Say, Has the cloister more like you?

FRIAR.   Don't know.
I must obey, dear sir.

TEMPLAR.   And you obey
Without much questioning?

FRIAR.   Would it else be

Obedience, dear sir?

TEMPLAR *(aside).*   Upon my soul,
Simplicity is always right. *(Aloud.)* No doubt
You may reveal to me who is so eager
To know me better?—Not yourself, I'll swear.   30

FRIAR. Would such a wish become or profit me?

TEMPLAR. Whom does it then become and profit, whom,
To be so curious?

FRIAR.   The Patriarch,
I must believe.—For it was he who sent me.

TEMPLAR. The Patriarch! Knows he no better, then,
Red cross on mantle white?

FRIAR.   I know it well!

TEMPLAR. Well, brother, well?—I am a Templar knight;
And captive—Further: taken at Tebnín,*
The fort we thought to scale ere truce's end
To march forthwith on Sidon;**—if I add: 40
As one of twenty taken and alone
By Saladin left living: then he knows,
Your Patriarch, all that he needs to know;—
More than he needs.

FRIAR.   . .But hardly more, I think,
Than he knows now.—He'd also like to know
Wherefore my lord by Saladin was spared;
Just he alone.

TEMPLAR.   Do I know that?—Already
My neck was bared, I knelt upon my cloak,
The blow awaiting: keenly Saladin

---

* A fortress north of Ptolemais, about fifteen miles from Tyre.
** A town on the Mediterranean.

Observes my face, leaps toward me, makes a sign. 50
They lift me up; I am unbound; I seek
To thank him; see his eyes in tears: but mute
Is he, am I; he goes, I stay.—And how
All that's connected, let the Patriarch
Himself unriddle.

FRIAR.   From it he concludes
That God for great and greater things must have
Preserved you.

TEMPLAR.   Yes, for mighty things indeed!
To save a Jewess from the fire; to guide
To Sinai* curious pilgrims; and the like.

FRIAR. That's to be seen! But so far not so bad.   60
Perhaps the Patriarch himself meanwhile
Has more important business for my lord.

TEMPLAR. You think so, brother?—Has he given you
hints
Already?

FRIAR.   Yes, indeed!—All I should do
Is first sound out my lord, to see if he
Might be the man.

TEMPLAR.   Why, well; go on and sound!
(Aside.) I wonder how he'll do this sounding.—
    (Aloud.) Well?

FRIAR. The quickest course will be to say right out
Just what the Patriarch wants.

TEMPLAR.   Good!

FRIAR.   He would ask
My lord to bear a letter.   70

TEMPLAR.   Me? But I'm

* Mt. Sinai, supposed to be the Biblical Mt. Horeb; as it is far
from Jerusalem, the Templar would have been gone a long
time.

No messenger.—And that should be a task
More glorious far than saving Jewish maidens
From death by fire?
FRIAR.   It must be so!—For—says
The Patriarch—upon this letter hangs
For all of Christendom a mighty weight.
To have delivered it in safety—says
The Patriarch—will one day bring the bearer
A special crown in Heaven as reward.
And of this crown—so says the Patriarch—
No man is worthier than my lord.   80
TEMPLAR.   Than I?
FRIAR. For to deserve this crown in Heaven—says
The Patriarch—there's scarce another man
More skillful than my lord.
TEMPLAR.   Than I?
FRIAR.   He says
You're free; can look about you everywhere;
You know how cities can be stormed and how
Defended; can—so says the Patriarch—
Best estimate the strength and weakness of
The wall most lately built by Saladin,
The inner, second wall, most vividly
Describe it—says the Patriarch—to all   90
The host of God.
TEMPLAR.   Good brother, if I but
Could know the detailed content of the note.
FRIAR. Ah that—I do not know so very well.
However, it is written to King Philip.*—
The Patriarch . . . I've often wondered how
A saint who lives in heaven otherwise

* Philip Augustus II of France (1165–1223), co-leader of the
Third Crusade with Richard I of England.

Can condescend to be so well informed
On worldly things. That must seem bitter to him.
TEMPLAR. Well then? The Patriarch?
FRIAR.   Knows through and through,
  Reliably, just how and in what strength,   100
  From what direction Saladin, in case
  The war breaks out again, will open up
  His own campaign.
TEMPLAR.   He knows that?
FRIAR.   Yes, and wants
  To let King Philip know it: so that he
  Might estimate the danger, if it be
  So great that at all costs the armistice,
  Which your great Order nobly violated,
  He should restore with Saladin.
TEMPLAR.   Ah ha!
  Ah what a Patriarch!—This bold, good man
  Would make of me no common agent, but—   110
  A spy.—Good brother, tell your Patriarch,
  So far as you could sound me out, that this
  Was not the task for me.—Say that I must
  Regard myself as captive still; and that
  The Templars' only calling is to use
  The sword to smite, and not to act the spy.
FRIAR. I thought as much!—Nor am I much inclined
  To chide my lord for it.—Though, to be sure,
  The best is yet to come.—The Patriarch
  Has wormed it out, the name and the location 120
  Of that stronghold on Lebanon,* wherein
  Are kept the monstrous sums of gold with which
  The Sultan's cautious father pays the troops

---

* A mountain range close to the Mediterranean in the (present) Lebanese Republic.

And other costs of war. From time to time
On hidden paths the Sultan to this fort
Betakes himself, but scantily attended.
You follow?

TEMPLAR.   Never, never!

FRIAR.   What would be
More simple than to seize the Sultan's person?
To make an end of him?—You shudder?—O,
A pair of pious Maronites * have offered
To dare the deed, if there's a doughty man
To lead them on.

TEMPLAR.   And so your Patriarch
Has chosen me to be that doughty man?

FRIAR. He thinks King Philip out of Ptolemais **
Might send his men to lend a hand.

TEMPLAR.   To me?
Me, brother, me? Have you not heard just now
What gratitude I owe to Saladin?

FRIAR. I have indeed.

TEMPLAR.   And yet?

FRIAR.   O well—so says
The Patriarch—that's very fine; but God,
Your Order . . .   140

TEMPLAR.   Alter nought! Require of me
No knavish trick!

FRIAR.   Of course not!—Only—says
The Patriarch—what seems a knavish trick
To human eyes may not seem so to God.

TEMPLAR. Then I should owe to Saladin my life

---

* A Syrian Christian sect founded in the 7th century; their
central seat is still Mt. Lebanon.
** Ptolemais, another name for (Saint-Jean-d') Acre, a strong
fortress on the Bay of Acre.

And take his from him?

FRIAR.   Faugh!—and yet—so says
The Patriarch—still Saladin remains
A foe of Christendom, hence may not claim
The right to be your friend.

TEMPLAR.   How friend? To whom
I merely would not play the thankless villain?

FRIAR. Quite true!—And yet—so says the
Patriarch—   150
We are absolved of thanks, 'fore God and men,
If for *our* sake the service was not done.
And since it's rumored—says the Patriarch—
The Sultan had not spared your life unless
In your expression, in your very being,
Some semblance of his brother struck his eye . . .

TEMPLAR. The Patriarch knows this too, and all the
same . . . ?
Ah, were that definite! Ah, Saladin!
What? Nature should have shaped one single trait
In me that had your brother's form: to which   160
There were no correspondence in my soul?
This correspondence I could then suppress
To please a Patriarch?—No, Nature, no!
Thou'rt not so false! God does not contradict
Himself so in His works!—Go, brother, now.
Do not stir up the gall in me!—Go! go!

FRIAR. I go; and go more cheerful than I came.
My lord should pardon me. We cloister folk
Are under rule, we must obey the heads.

SCENE 6

(Daya, who has been observing the Templar for some time from a distance, now approaches him.)

DAYA *(aside)*. The friar, it seems, left him in no good
  mood.

  But I must risk my errand.

TEMPLAR.   Excellent!—

  How true the ancient saw, that monk and woman
  Are as the devil's claws, alike and paired.
  Today he passes me from one to the other.

DAYA. What do I see?—You, noble knight?—Thank
  God

  A thousand times!—O speak, where have you been
  In all this time?—I hope you've not been sick?

TEMPLAR. No.

DAYA.   Quite, quite well?

TEMPLAR.   Yes.

DAYA.   We were so concerned
  On your account.   10

TEMPLAR.   You were?

DAYA.   No doubt you were
  Away?

TEMPLAR. You've guessed it.

DAYA.   Just returned today?

TEMPLAR. No, yesterday.

DAYA.   And Rachel's father too
  Has just returned. So may she now have hope?

TEMPLAR. Of what?

DAYA.   Of what so oft she begged of you.
  Her father will invite you now himself
  Most urgently. He comes from Babylon;
  With twenty fully laden camels, with
  Whatever of precious spices, jewels, stuffs,
  That India, Persia, Syria, even China,
  Esteem of highest worth.   20

TEMPLAR.   I purchase nothing.

DAYA. His people honor him as though a prince.
  But that they speak of Nathan as the Wise
  And not the Rich, I've often thought that strange.
TEMPLAR. Perhaps they think that wise and rich are
  one.
DAYA. But most of all they should have called him
  good.
  For you cannot conceive how good he is.
  When he was told what Rachel owes to you:
  What had he, in that moment, failed to do
  And give to you!
TEMPLAR.   Well!
DAYA.   Try it, come and see!
TEMPLAR. See what? How quick a moment's time is
  fled?   30
DAYA. Had I, if he were not so good, myself
  Put up with him so long? Do you suppose
  I do not feel my worth as Christian woman?
  It was not sung to me as cradle-song
  That one day I'd accompany my husband
  To Palestine for only this one end:
  To rear a Jewish maiden. For my husband
  In Emperor Fredrick's * army was a noble.
  Esquire—
TEMPLAR. By birth a Swiss, who had the grace,
  And honor too, within the selfsame stream   40
  To drown with his Imperial Majesty.—
  Woman! How often have I heard all this?
  Will you then never cease thus to pursue me?
DAYA. Pursue you! gracious God!
TEMPLAR.   Yes, yes, pursue me.

  * Friedrich Barbarossa (1123–1190), one of the leaders of the
Third Crusade.

Once and for all, I won't see you again.
Nor hear you! Will not endless have recalled
A deed to which I gave no thought; and which,
When I reflect, makes of myself a riddle.
It's true, I'd not regret it. But look here:
If such a case recurs, then you're to blame   50
If I should act less quickly; should first off
Inquire a bit—and then let burn what burns.

DAYA. Now God forbid!

TEMPLAR.   Henceforth I beg at least
You'll know me not. This I request. And keep
The father off. For Jew is Jew. And I'm
A Swabian * blunt. The image of the girl
Has long since left my spirit; if indeed
It once was there.

DAYA.   But yours has not left *her*.

TEMPLAR. What good can that do? Tell me that.

DAYA.   Who knows?
For people are not always what they seem.   60

TEMPLAR. But rarely are they better. *(Starts off.)*

DAYA.   Wait a bit!
Why hasten?

TEMPLAR. Woman, do not make these palms to me
Repellent, since I love to walk beneath them.

DAYA. Then go, you German bear! then go!—*(Aside.)*
    And yet
I must not risk to lose the creature's trail.
(She follows him at a distance.)

* Popular tradition in Germany makes fun of the Swa-
bians (Schwaben), calling them honest but blunt and stupid.

ACT II

SCENE 1

(The Sultan's palace. Saladin and Sittah are at chess.*)

SITTAH. Where are you, Saladin? And how you play!
SALADIN. Not well? I thought.
SITTAH.   Quite well for me, perhaps.
   Take back that move.
SALADIN.   What for?
SITTAH.   That leaves your knight
   Uncovered.
SALADIN. True. Try that!
SITTAH.   I take it with
   My pawn.
SALADIN. That's true again.—Then check!
SITTAH.   What good
   Is that? I shield my king, like this: and you
   Are as you were.
SALADIN.   This is a squeeze, I see,
   From which I can't escape without some loss.
   Oh well! Then take the knight.
SITTAH.   I'd rather not.
   I'll pass him by.   10
SALADIN.   You give me nothing, find
   Your plan of greater value than my knight.
SITTAH. May be.
SALADIN. But reckon not without your host.
   For, look! This move you hardly could foresee?
SITTAH. Not I indeed. Could I foresee that you
   Would be so weary of your queen?

---

* Saladin is known to have been passionately fond of chess.

32

SALADIN.   My queen!

SITTAH. It's plain to see: today I win my thousand
   Dinars, * and not a farthing more.

SALADIN.   How so?

SITTAH. You ask?—Because you're simply bent on los-
     ing.
   Let's set aside the fact that such a game
   Is not the most enjoyable to play: 20
   Did I not always win the most with you
   When I was loser? Did you ever fail
   To pay the stake twofold, to comfort me
   For losing it?

SALADIN.   Well, well! So, I suppose,
   You lost on purpose when you lost, my sister?

SITTAH. At least this may be said: your open hand
   Prevents me from improving on my game.

SALADIN. But we forget our playing. Make an end!

SITTAH. You will it so? Well, check! and double
     check!

SALADIN. Ah ha, that second check I did not see,   30
   Which at the same time overthrows my queen.

SITTAH. Could that have been averted? Let me see.

SALADIN. No; no; just take the queen. I never was
   Too lucky with that piece.

SITTAH.   The playing-piece
   Alone?

SALADIN. Away with it!—That does no harm.
   For now again my cover is complete.

SITTAH. My brother has instructed me too well (*She
   leaves the queen.*)

---

* Dinar (from Latin *denarius*) was a gold coin, first minted in
the 7th century, which was for some centuries the Moslem
dollar, so to speak.

How courteously one should behave with queens.

SALADIN. Take it or not! For now I have no queen.

SITTAH. Why should I take it? Check! and check!   40

SALADIN.   Keep on.

SITTAH. And Check!—and check!—and check!

SALADIN.   And mate!

SITTAH.   Not quite;
    You move the knight between; or what you will.
    All one!

SALADIN. Quite right!—For you have won: and now
    Al-Hafi pays.—Bid him be summoned! quick!—
    You were not so mistaken, Sittah; I
    Was absent-minded, lost track of the game.
    And then: who'll always give us neutral * pieces
    Which nought recall and nothing designate?
    And was it with the Imam ** I was playing?—
    Oh pshaw! A loss demands excuse. Not just   50
    The shapeless pieces, Sittah, can account
    For my defeat: your calm and rapid glance,
    Your skill . . .

SITTAH.   Even so your only purpose is
    To blunt the sting of loss. Enough, you were
    Distracted; more than I.

SALADIN.   Than you? What should
    Distract *your* mind?

SITTAH.   Not your distraction, truly!—
    When shall we play so zealously again?!

SALADIN. Why, then we'll play so much the lustier!—
    Ah! since the war begins again?—Well, let it!—

* Lessing thought Mohammedans were forbidden to use chessmen which represented men or animals.

** Imam is the priest who conducts the service in a mosque; he would be sure to insist on the use of plain chessmen.

Come on!—It was not I who drew the sword;   60
I'd have renewed the armistice; and gladly
In this way I had given a proper husband
To Sittah. Richard's * brother he must be:
He is the one.

SITTAH.   If you can only praise
Your Richard!

SALADIN.   If our brother Melek ** then
Were given Richard's sister for his wife:
Ha, what a house we'd have! Of all the first,
Best houses in the world, the very best!—
You see I am not slow to praise myself.
I think that I deserve the friends I have.—   70
What men would have been born to them, what
    men!

SITTAH. Did I not smile at once at your fine dream?
You do not know the Christians, will not know
    them.
Their pride is to be Christians, and not men.
For even that which from their Founder's day
With human nature spices superstition
They don't love for its human worth: because
Their Jesus taught it, by him it was done.—
O well for them, that he was a good man!
And well for them, that they can take his virtue   80
On faith!—But what of virtue?—It's not that
Shall overspread the world, but just his name;
That name shall swallow all the names of men,

---

* Richard I of England, called "Coeur de Lion" (1157–99),
set out for the Third Crusade in 1191. He and Saladin had
great admiration for each other. History knows nothing of a
plan to marry his brother to Sittah.
** Richard proposed in 1191 that Saladin's brother Melek
should marry his widowed sister Joan, queen of Sicily.

    Put them to shame. The name, the name alone,
    Is all they care for.

SALADIN.   Otherwise you'd wonder
    Why they should ask that you and Melek both
    Should bear the name of Christians, ere you might
    Have Christians as your wedded lovers?

SITTAH.   Yes!
    Why is it only Christians who may claim
    The love that God bestows on man and wo-
    man?   90

SALADIN. O, they believe such childishnesses that
    It's not too hard to think this one among them.—
    And yet you're wrong.—The Templars are to
    blame,
    And not the Christians; are to blame as Templars,
    And not as Christians. For through them alone
    Our project came to nought. The town of Acre,
    Which Richard's sister was to bring as dowry
    To brother Melek, they will not give up.
    To keep the knight's advantage out of danger,
    They act the monk, the silly monk. In hope   100
    Of playing us a clever trick, they would
    Not wait until the armistice should end.—
    Fine doings! Keep right on, good sirs, keep on!—
    I'm quite content!—Were all else as it should be!

SITTAH. What else disturbs you? What else could there
    be
    To rob you of composure?

SALADIN.   What so long
    Has robbed me of composure, now and ever.—
    I was at Lebanon to visit father.
    I fear he will succumb to care . . .

SITTAH.   O dear!   109

SALADIN. He can't hold out, is pinched on every hand;
　There's lack now here, now there—
SITTAH.　　　　　　　　　　What pinches, lacks?
SALADIN. What else but what I hardly deign to name?
　Which, when I have it, seems superfluous,
　And, when I lack it, indispensable.—
　Where is Al-Hafi now? Has no one gone
　To look for him?—Accursed, wretched money!—
　(Enter Al-Hafi.) Al-Hafi, welcome.

SCENE 2

AL-HAFI.　　　　　　　　Sultan, I presume
　The moneys due from Egypt have arrived.
　I hope there's much.
SALADIN.　　　　　　Have you some news?
AL-HAFI.　　　　　　　　　　　What, I?
　I thought I should receive some here.
SALADIN.　　　　　　　　　　You'll pay
　Sittah a thousand dinars. *(Abstractedly walking up
　and down.)*
AL-HAFI.　　　　　　Pay! not get!
　O fine! For something that is less than nothing.—
　To Sittah?—her again? For a lost game?—
　Again a loss at chess?—The board still stands!
SITTAH. You don't grudge me my luck?
AL-HAFI *(eyeing the board)*.　　What, grudge you—
　　if—
　You know the rest.　　　　　　　　　　　10
SITTAH *(making a sign)*. Pst! Hafi! pst!
AL-HAFI *(still eyeing the board)*.　　Don't grudge
　It to yourself.
SITTAH.　　　　Al-Hafi, pst!

AL-HAFI *(to Sittah)*.   The whites
  Were yours? You're checking?
SITTAH *(aside)*.   Good, he has not heard.
AL-HAFI. Now it's his turn to play?
SITTAH *(advancing)*.   You are to tell me
  That I can get my money.
AL-HAFI *(still intent on the game)*. Yes; you shall
  Receive it now as always.
SITTAH.   Are you mad?
AL-HAFI. The game is not yet up. Look, Saladin,
  You have not lost.
SALADIN *(scarcely listening)*. O yes I have! Just pay!
AL-HAFI. Just pay and pay! Your queen is standing
    there.
SALADIN *(as before)*. No matter; she's not in the game.
SITTAH.   Be quick
  And say that I can have the money fetched.   20
AL-HAFI *(still immersed in the game)*.
  Of course, the same as always.—All the same;
  And even if the queen is gone; you are
  Not mate on that account.
SALADIN *(steps up and overturns the board)*. I am; and
    want
  It so.
AL-HAFI. Oh ho!—Game like to winnings! And
  Paid just as won.
SALADIN *(to Sittah)*. What does he say? What's this?
SITTAH *(motioning from time to time to Hafi)*.
  You know his way. He likes to balk; he likes
  To be requested; feels a little envy.—
SALADIN. But not of you? Not of my sister, h'm?
  What is this, Hafi? Envy? you?
AL-HAFI.   May be!

May be!—I'd like to have her brain myself;   30
Would like to be as good as she.

SITTAH.   Meanwhile
He's always paid me promptly up to now.
And he will pay today. Just let him be!—
So go, Al-Hafi, go! Be sure I'll have
The money fetched.

AL-HAFI.   No, no; I'll play no more
This masquerade. For he must soon or late
Be told the truth.

SALADIN.   Who must? and what?

SITTAH.   Al-Hafi!
Is this your promise? Thus you keep your word?

AL-HAFI. How could I think that it would go so far?

SALADIN. Shall I learn nothing, then?   40

SITTAH.   I beg, Al-Hafi,
Be modest.

SALADIN.   This is strange! What could my Sittah
So solemnly, so warmly of a stranger,
Yes, of a dervish, rather than of me,
Her brother, ask in secrecy? It's time
I should command, Al-Hafi.—Dervish, speak!

SITTAH. My brother, do not let a trifling thing
Come closer to your thought than it is worth.
You know that several times, in chess, I've won
The selfsame sum from you. And since I need
No money now; and since in Hafi's fund   50
The money's not too plentiful; why then
These items were not cashed. But have no fear!
You shall not have them, brother, nor Al-Hafi,
Nor yet the treasury.

AL-HAFI.   If that were all!

SITTAH. More of the same.—That too I have let stand

Which you had formerly to me allotted; that
I have not touched for several months.

AL-HAFI.   And still
Not all!

SALADIN. Not yet?—Then speak!

AL-HAFI.   Since we from Egypt
Expected money, she . . .

SITTAH.   Why listen to him?

AL-HAFI. Not only has had nothing . . .   60

SALADIN.   Noble girl!
But has advanced her own as well. Not so?

AL-HAFI. Maintained your court; all your expenditure
Herself has paid.

SALADIN.   Ha, there I see my sister! *(Embracing her.)*

SITTAH. Who had enriched me so, save you, my
brother,
That I could do this thing?

AL-HAFI.   I think he will
Make her as beggar-poor as he's become.

SALADIN. I poor? her brother poor? When had I more?
When less in hand?—*One* dress, *one* sword, *one*
horse—
And then *one* God! What need have I of more?
And when can I lack that? And yet, Al-Hafi,   70
I still might chide you.

SITTAH.   Brother, do not chide!
Had I such power to lighten Father's cares!

SALADIN. Oh, Oh! You swiftly beat my joyousness
To earth again!—To me, for me, there lacks
No thing, nor can.—But he is lacking all,
And thus we lack it too.—What shall I do?—
From Egypt we may long get nothing yet.

God knows the cause; for all is quiet there.—
I'll gladly scrimp, retrench, and save, if only
I am alone affected, and no other   80
Need suffer want.—But what does that avail?
One horse, one dress, one sword I have to have.
Nor is there any haggling with my God.
For as it is he is content with little:
This heart of mine.—Upon the overflow,
Al-Hafi, of your funds I'd firmly reckoned.

AL-HAFI. The overflow?—Confess: would you have
    failed
    To have me spitted, throttled at the least,
    Had you found overflow with me? Embezzlement,
    That I could risk.   90

SALADIN.   Well, now, what's to be done?—
    Could you, to start with, draw on no one else
    But Sittah?

SITTAH.   Would I have relinquished, brother,
    This prior right? To Hafi? Even now
    I claim it still. For I am not as yet
    Quite high and dry.

SALADIN.   Not high and dry as yet!
    That tops it all!—Go, Hafi, lay your plans!
    Take money whence you can! and as you can!
    Go, borrow, promise.—Only borrow not
    Of those I have enriched. For borrowing
    Of those might mean that I demand return.   100
    Go to the stingiest; they'll lend to me
    Most readily. For they are sure to know
    How fast their money doubles in my hands.

AL-HAFI. I know no one like that.

SITTAH.   I just recall
    A rumor that your friend has now returned.

AL-HAFI *(startled)*. My friend? Who should that be?
SITTAH.   I mean the Jew
  You praise so highly.
AL-HAFI.   Praise a Jew? and highly?
SITTAH. A Jew to whom—I still recall quite well
  The words you used of him—his God had given,
  Of all the goods of earth, in fullest measure,   110
  The greatest and the least.
AL-HAFI.   What, said I so?—
  What did I mean by that?
SITTAH.   The smallest: wealth.
  The greatest: wisdom.
AL-HAFI.   This about a Jew?
  About a Jew you say I used these words?
SITTAH. You did not speak to me so of your Nathan?
AL-HAFI. Ah ha! of him! Of Nathan!—I admit
  I had forgotten him.—What, really? He
  Is home again at last? Well, well! Why then,
  He's likely not so badly off.—Quite right:
  The people used to call him wise. And rich.   120
SITTAH. The rich they call him more than ever now.
  The town is ringing with reports of all
  The treasures and the jewels he has brought.
AL-HAFI. Well, if he's rich again, without a doubt
  He's wise again as well.
SITTAH.   What say you, Hafi,
  Suppose you went to him?
AL-HAFI.   You mean to say:
  To borrow of him?—Ah, if you but knew him!
  He, lend?—Why, never to lend is just his wisdom.
SITTAH. You drew me once a very different picture.
AL-HAFI. Why, he might lend you goods, perhaps.
  But money?   130

Not money, ever.—True, he's such a Jew,
As you'll not often find. He has good sense;
Good manners, too; can play chess well. And yet
Stands out from other Jews no less in evil
Than in the good.—You must not count on him.—
He does give to the poor; perhaps as well
As Saladin. If not as much: at least
As willingly. Yet quite without pretense.
And Mussulman * and Parsee,** Jew and Christian,
He treats alike.   140
SITTAH.   And such a man . . .
SALADIN.   How comes it,
    That of this man I never heard?
SITTAH.   And he
    Would lend not to the Sultan, not to him,
    Who only needs for others, not himself?
AL-HAFI. Now there again you see the Jew in him;
    The common Jew!—Believe me!—For he is
    So envious, so jealous about giving,
    That every 'God reward you' in the world
    He'd like to claim himself. And that is why
    He lends to none, that he may always have
    Something to give. Since generosity   150
    Is ordered in his law, not courteousness:
    His generous giving makes of him the most
    Discourteous fellow in the world. I grant
    Of late I've slightly fallen out with him;
    But think not that I'd fail to do him justice.
    He's good in all things, only not in that;
    Not that indeed. I'll hasten off at once

    * Another term for Moslem, Mohammedan.
    ** An adherent of the ancient Persian religion called Zoro-
astrian; they were fire-worshippers.

And knock at other doors . . . For I recall
A certain Moor, who's rich and stingy too.
I go; I go. *(He hurries out).*   160
SITTAH.   Why hurry, Hafi?
SALADIN.   Let him!

SCENE 3

(Sittah. Saladin.)

SITTAH. He hastes as though evading me!—Now what
   Is this?—Has he been actually deceived—
   Or—would he just mislead us?
SALADIN.   Can I tell?
   I scarcely know of whom you spoke; and of
   Your Jew, your Nathan, never heard till now.
SITTAH. Why, can it be that such a man remained
   Concealed from you, of whom the people say
   He's found the graves of Solomon and David
   And by a secret, mighty word has power
   To break their seals? And thence from time   10
      to time
   He brings to light the immeasurable wealth
   Which could proclaim no lesser source?
SALADIN.   If truly
   This man derives his wealth from graves, be sure
   It's not from Solomon's nor David's, where
   Poor fools lie buried!
SITTAH.   Yes, or miscreants!
   And of his wealth the source is richer far,
   More copious, than graves all full of gold.
SALADIN. For he's a trader; so I hear.
SITTAH.   In truth,

His beasts of burden travel all the roads,
Traverse all deserts; and in all the ports   20
At anchor lie his vessels. Formerly
Al-Hafi told me this; and with delight
He added, with what great nobility
His friend bestowed what he did not disdain
With zeal and shrewdness daily to acquire;
Added, how free his mind of prejudice;
His heart how open unto every virtue,
With every beauty perfectly attuned.

SALADIN. Yet now Al-Hafi spoke so dubiously,
So coldly of him.   30

SITTAH.   No, not cold; embarrassed.
As if he thought it dangerous to praise him,
And yet he would not chide him undeserved.—
Or is it really true that even the best
Among a people never quite escapes
That people's traits? that Hafi should have cause
In this regard to deprecate his friend?—
Well, be that as it may!—Suppose the Jew
Be more or less the Jew: if he be rich,
Enough for us!

SALADIN.   I hope you would not take
His property by force?   40

SITTAH.   What does that mean,
By force? With fire and sword? No, no, what need
With weaklings any force but their own weak-
    ness?—
Come with me to my harem for a while,
To hear a singing girl that I've just bought.
Meanwhile perhaps I'll ripen a design
I have for trying on this Nathan.—Come!

SCENE 4

(In front of Nathan's house, adjacent to the palms. Rachel and Nathan come out of the house. Daya joins them.)

RACHEL. You've tarried very long, dear father; now
    He'll hardly be here any more.
NATHAN.   Oh well;
    If here beneath the palms no longer, then
    Some other place.—Be not disturbed.—But look!
    Is that not Daya coming toward us?
RACHEL.   Surely
    She will have lost him.
NATHAN.   Or as surely not.
RACHEL. Else she'd come faster.
NATHAN.   She's not seen us yet . . .
RACHEL. She sees us now.
NATHAN.   Is walking twice as fast.
    But do be calm, be calm!
RACHEL.   Would you prefer
    A daughter that was calm in such a case?   10
    Untroubled as to him whose benefaction
    Had meant her life? Her life—to her so dear
    Because she owes it first of all to you.
NATHAN. I would not have you other than you are:
    Not if I knew that in your soul were stirring
    A wholly different thing.
RACHEL.   What, father, what?
NATHAN. You ask me that? So timid still? Whatever
    Goes on in you is innocence and nature.
    So let it cause you no concern. To me

It causes none. But promise me, my child: 20
That when your heart one day declares itself
More audibly, you will conceal from me
None of its wishes.
RACHEL.   Just the very thought
I might prefer concealment makes me tremble.
NATHAN. No more of this! For that, once and for all,
Is settled now.—And here is Daya.—Well?
DAYA. He still is strolling here beneath the palms;
And must at once appear around that wall.—
See, there he comes.
RACHEL.   Ah, seems irresolute:
Where to? keep on? go down? turn right? turn
    left?   30
DAYA. No, no; he'll make the circuit of the cloister
Again, I'm sure; then he must pass this spot.
Agreed?
RACHEL.   That's right!—And have you talked with
    him
Already? How's his mood today?
DAYA.   As ever.
NATHAN. See to it then that he does not perceive
You here. Step back more. Better go inside.
RACHEL. Just one more look!—That hedge, that steals
    him from me!
DAYA. Come, come! Your father's right. You run the
    risk
That if he sees you he will turn around.
RACHEL. The wretched hedge!   40
NATHAN.   And if he should emerge
Quite suddenly from it, he needs must see you.
So get you gone!

DAYA.   Come, come! I know a window,
  From which we can observe them.
RACHEL.   What? you do? *(They go in.)*

SCENE 5

(Nathan. Templar.)

NATHAN. I almost shrink from this strange man. Recoil
  Almost before his rugged virtue. How
  Can one be so embarrassed by a man?
  Look! there he comes! By Heaven! There's a youth
  Might be a man! I like it well, that glance,
  So good, defiant! and that sturdy stride!
  Only the shell is bitter, and the core
  Is sweet and good.—Where have I seen the like?—
  Your pardon, noble Frank * . . .
TEMPLAR.   What?
NATHAN.   Pray permit . . .
TEMPLAR. Permit what, Jew?   10
NATHAN.   That I should be so bold
  As to address you.
TEMPLAR.   Can I stop you? Yet
  Be brief.
NATHAN.   Delay, and hasten not so fast,
  Nor so contemptuously, to shun a man
  Whom you have put forever in your debt.
TEMPLAR. How so?—I almost guess. Not so? You
  are . . .
NATHAN. My name is Nathan; I'm the maiden's father,
  Whom your great heart delivered from the flames;
  I come . . .

  * A term used in the Levant to designate any European.

TEMPLAR.   Why, if to thank me:—stop! I have
  Endured already for this trifling thing
  Too many thanks.—And you especially   20
  Owe me no thanks at all. For did I know
  This girl to be your daughter? We are charged,
  As Templars, to rush forward to the aid
  Of anyone we see in some distress.
  Besides, my life was burdensome to me
  At just that moment. Very willingly
  I seized the chance to throw it in the breach
  To save another—were it nothing but
  A Jewish maiden's life.
NATHAN.   Great! Great and monstrous!—
  And yet I catch your drift. A modest greatness   30
  Would hide behind the monstrous, merely to
  Escape from admiration.—But if it
  Thus scorns the gift of open admiration,
  What sort of gift would it less quickly scorn?—
  Sir Knight, were you no stranger here, nor yet
  A prisoner, less boldly I would ask.
  So speak, command: wherewith can you be served?
TEMPLAR. By you? With nought.
NATHAN.   I am a wealthy man.
TEMPLAR. I never thought the richer Jew the better.
NATHAN. Is that a reason why you should not use   40
  The better thing he owns: his wealth?
TEMPLAR.   All right
  I'll not refuse, for my poor mantle's sake.
  So soon as it is wholly worn and torn,
  And will not suffer either stitch or patch,
  I'll come to you and borrow for a new one,
  Or cloth or cash.—Put off that darkling look!
  And yet you're safe; as yet it's not worn out.

You see: it's still in fairly decent shape.
Just that one tip there has a filthy spot,
For it is singed; that happened when I bore   50
Your daughter through the fire.
NATHAN *(seizing the tip and eyeing it).* I find it
    strange
    That such an ugly spot, soiled by the fire,
    Bears better witness than a man's own lips.
    I'd like to kiss it now—that spot!—Forgive!—
    That was not meant.
TEMPLAR.   What?
NATHAN.   Why, a tear fell on it.
TEMPLAR. No harm! It has had other drops. *(Aside.)*
    But soon
    This Jew will put me in confusion.
NATHAN.   Would
    You be so kind as send once to my daughter
    Your mantle?
TEMPLAR.   What to do?
NATHAN.   That she as well
    May press her lips upon this spot. For she,   60
    I think, must hope in vain to clasp your knees.
TEMPLAR. But, Jew—your name is Nathan?—Really,
    Nathan—
    You   choose   your   words   most—well—most
        pointedly—
    I am perplexed.—You speak the truth—I had . . .
NATHAN. Guise and disguise you, as you will. And still
    I'll find you out.—You were too good, too honest,
    To be more courtly.—There the maiden, all
    Emotion; here her female agent, all
    Submissiveness; the father far away—

You were concerned for her good name; you fled 70
Temptation; fled, in order not to conquer.
For that I thank you too—
TEMPLAR.   I must confess,
You know just how the Templars ought to think.
NATHAN. Templars alone? and merely *ought?* and
          merely,
Because the Order's rules command it so?
I know how good men think; I know as well
That all lands bear good men.
TEMPLAR.   But different,
You grant?
NATHAN.   Oh yes: in color, dress, and shape.
TEMPLAR. And more or less in one land than the other.
NATHAN. This difference is not large. For every-
          where   80
The great man needs much room; and several,
Too closely planted, break each other's limbs.
The middling sort, like you and me, are found
In numbers everywhere you care to look.
Only, the one must not carp at the other.
Only, the club must put up with the stick;
Only, a hillock must not make pretense
That it alone rose out of mother earth.
TEMPLAR. Well said indeed!—But do you know the
          folk
That was the first to carp at other tribes?   90
Was first to call itself the chosen people?
Suppose that I did not exactly hate,
But for its pride was forced to scorn that folk:
The pride it then passed on to Christians, Moslem,
Which says their god alone is the true god!

You're startled at this from a Christian Templar?
But when and where has pious frenzy, claiming
The better god, intent on forcing him
Upon the world at large, revealed itself
In blacker form than here, and now? O he   100
Whose eyes drop not their present scales . . . And
     yet
Be blind who will!—Forget what I have said;
And leave me! *(Starts to go.)*
NATHAN.   Ha! You know not how much closer
I now shall cling to you.—O come, we must,
We must be friends!—Disdain my folk, as much
As ever you will. For neither one has chosen
His folk. Are we our folk? What is a folk?
Are Jew and Christian sooner Jew and Christian
Than man? How good, if I have found in you
One more who is content to bear the name   110
Of man!
TEMPLAR. By Heaven, yes! you have indeed!
You have in truth!—Your hand—I am ashamed,
To have misjudged you for a moment's time.
NATHAN. And I am proud of it. It's only baseness
That rarely is misjudged.
TEMPLAR.   And what is rare
We hardly can forget.—Yes, Nathan, yes:
We must, we must become good friends.
NATHAN.   We are
So now.—How happy will my Rachel be!—
And what a cheerful prospect opens out
Before my eyes!—Ah, wait until you know
     her!   120
TEMPLAR. I burn with eagerness.—Who rushes there
Out of your house? I think it is her Daya?

NATHAN. Quite right. So anxiously?
TEMPLAR.   Our Rachel has
  Not met with harm, I hope?

SCENE 6

DAYA. *(Enter Daya in haste.)* Oh Nathan, Nathan!
NATHAN. Well?
DAYA.   Pardon, noble knight, that I'm compelled
  To interrupt.
NATHAN.   What is it, then?
TEMPLAR.   What is it?
DAYA. The Sultan sends for you. The Sultan would
  Have speech with you; O God!
NATHAN.   The Sultan? me?
  No doubt he's curious to see himself
  The novelties I've brought. Send word and say
  As yet I have unpacked but little, nothing.
DAYA. No, no; he would see nothing; would consult
  you,
  Yourself, he said, as soon as ever you can.   10
NATHAN. Say I shall come.—Go back then quickly,
  go!
DAYA. O take this not amiss, most honored knight.—
  O dear, we're so distressed, we cannot think
  What he can want.
NATHAN.   That will be shown. Go, go!
                              (Exit Daya.)

SCENE 7

TEMPLAR. You do not know him yet?—I mean, in
  person?

NATHAN. Whom, Saladin? Not yet. Though I have
    not
  Avoided him, I have not sought to know him.
  For common talk spoke far too well of him
  That I'd not rather trust it than to see.
  But now—assuming that it's true—if he
  By sparing of your life . . .
TEMPLAR.   Indeed, so much
  Is really true. The present life I live
  He gave to me.
NATHAN.   And by that gift to me
  A double, triple life. This fact has changed   10
  All things between us; has around me cast
  A rope that binds me henceforth to his service.
  I scarce, yes, scarce, can now await what he
  Will first require of me. I am prepared
  For everything; prepared as well to say
  That I am so because of you alone.
TEMPLAR. As yet I could not give him thanks myself,
  However often I might cross his path.
  The impress that I made upon him came
  As rapidly as then it disappeared.   20
  Who knows if he remembers my existence.
  And yet he must, for once at least, recall
  My person, make disposal of my fate.
  It's not enough that by his nod and will
  I'm still alive: from him I have to learn
  Whose will shall tell me how I am to live.
NATHAN. Quite right; so much the less will I delay.—
  A word may fall that offers me excuse
  To speak of you.—Forgive me, pray—I haste.—
  But when may we receive you in my house?   30

TEMPLAR. When you permit.

NATHAN.   No, when you will.

TEMPLAR.   Today.

NATHAN. Your name?—I have to ask.

TEMPLAR.   My name has been—
   Is Curt von Stauffen.—Curt.

NATHAN.   Von Stauffen?—Stauffen?

TEMPLAR. Why does that strike you so?

NATHAN.   Von Stauffen?—Surely
   Of that race there were more . . .

TEMPLAR.   O yes, out here
   A number now are rotting in the ground.
   My uncle too—my father, I should say—
   Why does your eye transfix me more and more?

NATHAN. It's nothing. I can't see enough of you.

TEMPLAR. Then I shall leave you first. The searcher's
    eye   40
   Not seldom finds more than he wished to find.
   I fear it, Nathan. Let the course of time,
   Not curious prying, make us better known. *(Exit.)*

NATHAN *(looking after him in astonishment).*
   "Not seldom has the searcher's eye found more
   Than he desired."—As if he'd read my soul!—
   Upon my word: that might befall me too.—
   It's Wolf in growth and gait: his voice as well.
   Precisely so he used to toss his head;
   Just so the sword lay on his arm; his brows
   Wolf used to stroke with leveled hand, as if   50
   To hide the deep-set fire within his eyes.—
   How such deep-graven images at times
   Can sleep in us, until a word or tone
   Arouses them.—Von Stauffen!—Yes, that's right;

Filnek and Stauffen; soon I will know more.
Our Daya—Well, come hither to me, Daya.

(Enter Daya.)

SCENE 8

NATHAN. I'll wager, both your hearts are overweighed
 With need to learn far other news than what
 The Sultan wants.
DAYA.   You don't take that amiss?
 You'd just begun to speak familiarly
 And kindly with him, when the Sultan's message
 Withdrew us from the window.
NATHAN.   Tell her, then,
 She may expect him any moment now.
DAYA. For sure? for sure?
NATHAN.   I hope I can rely
 Upon you, Daya? Be upon your guard,
 I beg of you; and you shall not regret it.   10
 Your conscience, too, shall find its recompense.
 I beg you only, do not spoil my plan.
 I beg you only, tell your tale and question
 Discreetly, with reserve . . .
DAYA.   To think that you
 Remember that!—I go; and you go too.
 For look! I really think that from the Sultan
 Another comes, Al-Hafi, yes, your dervish. *(Exit.)*

SCENE 9

AL-HAFI *(enters)*. Well, well, I was about to call
 on you.
NATHAN. Why all the haste? What does he want of
 me?

AL-HAFI. Who?

NATHAN. Saladin.—I come, I come.

AL-HAFI. To whom?
To Saladin?

NATHAN. Does he not send you?

AL-HAFI. Me?
No. Has he sent already?

NATHAN. Yes, of course.

AL-HAFI. Then that's correct.

NATHAN. Why, what's correct?

AL-HAFI. Oh, that . . .
I'm not to blame; God knows I'm not to blame.—
How much I said of you, what lies I told
To stave it off!

NATHAN. To stave what off?

AL-HAFI. Why, that
You've now become his treasurer. You have 10
My pity. But I will not see it done.
I go this moment; you've already heard
Whither I go; and know the way.—And if
You've messages to send along the way,
Then speak, I'm at your service. Yet it may
Not go beyond what nakedness can carry.
I go, so speak.

NATHAN. Al-Hafi, do remember
That not a word of this I know. So tell me
What you are babbling.

AL-HAFI. Surely you will take
Your purses with you? 20

NATHAN. Purses?

AL-HAFI. Yes, the cash
That you are to advance to Saladin.

NATHAN. And that is all it is?

AL-HAFI.   I should stand by
   And see him bleed you dry from top to toe?
   Watch wastefulness from those once bursting barns
   Of generosity just take and take,
   Till even the mice in them cannot but starve?
   Are you so simple as to think that one
   Who needs your cash will take your counsel too?—
   Oh, he, and counsel! When has Saladin
   Accepted such?—Imagine, Nathan, what   30
   Just now I suffered at his hands,
NATHAN.   Well, what?
AL-HAFI. I come to him, just after he has played
   Chess with his sister. Sittah's game's not bad;
   There stood the game, which Saladin believed
   Was lost, had given up, still on the board.
   I take a look at it, and see at once
   The game was far from lost.
NATHAN.   Well, what a find
   For you!
AL-HAFI. His king could be protected with a pawn
   Upon her check.—Could I but demonstrate   40
   The thing to you!
NATHAN.   Oh, I can well believe it.
AL-HAFI. For thus the rook had open file, and she
   Was done for.—This I'd like to show to him
   And called him.—Think!
NATHAN.   He shares not your opinion?
AL-HAFI. He doesn't even listen, in contempt
   He overturns the board.
NATHAN.   Can such things be?
AL-HAFI. And says, he simply *wants* it to be mate;
   He wants it! Is that playing?
NATHAN.   Hardly, no;

That's playing with the game.

AL-HAFI.   And yet the stake
   Was more than empty shells.   50

NATHAN.   Oh, money, bosh!
   That was the least. But not to let you speak!
   Upon a point of such importance, not
   To listen to you! and your eagle glance
   Not to admire! that calls for vengeance; h'm?

AL-HAFI. Nonsense! I only tell you this, that you
   Can see yourself the kind of mind he has.
   In short, I cannot bear it any longer.
   I have to run around to filthy Moors
   And ask and beg that one will lend him money.
   And I, who for myself have never begged,   60
   Must borrow now for others. Borrowing
   Is much the same as begging: just as lending,
   At usury, is much the same as stealing.
   Among my Ghebers,* on the Ganges, there
   I don't need either, and I need not be
   The tool of either. On the Ganges, now,
   There only men are found. Here, you alone
   Are worthy of our life upon the Ganges.—
   You'll go along?—Just leave him in the lurch
   With all this stuff he sets such store upon.   70
   He'll take it from you anyway in time.
   Join me, and forthwith all the worry's done.
   I'll get a gown for you. Come, come!

NATHAN.   I think
   That's something to fall back on. But, Al-Hafi,
   I'll think it over. Wait . . .

AL-HAFI.   You'll think it over?
   This cannot be thought over.

---

* Another term for Parsee, see note to p. 43.

NATHAN.   Wait until
  I come back from the Sultan; wait until
  I take my leave . . .
AL-HAFI.   To think things over, means
  To seek for reasons to refuse. And who
  Cannot resolve upon a moment's notice   80
  To live his own life, he forever lives
  A slave to others.—As you will!—Farewell!
  Do as you like.—My way lies there; yours here.
NATHAN. Al-Hafi! First you have to verify
  Your balance?
AL-HAFI.   Rubbish! All the residue
  In my account is not worth adding up;
  What's owing me, you'll guarantee—or Sittah.
  Farewell! *(exit.)*
NATHAN *(looking after him)*. I will!—So noble, wild,
    and good—
  What name for him?—I think, when all is said,
  The genuine beggar is the genuine king!
                      (Exit at the other side.)

ACT III

SCENE 1

(Nathan's house.)

RACHEL. How, Daya, did my father choose his words?
  "I might expect him any moment now?"
  That sounds—agreed?—as if he would appear
  At once—How many moments have gone by!—
  Ah well: who thinks of moments that are past?—
  I'll only live in each one as it comes.
  That moment must arrive which brings him too.
DAYA. O, out upon that message from the Sultan!
  Except for that I'm sure that Nathan would
  Have brought him straight to us.   10
RACHEL.   And when it has
  Arrived, that moment; and in consequence
  The warmest, deepest wish of mine has been
  Fulfilled: what then?—what then?
DAYA.   What then? Why then
  I hope *my* dearest wish may likewise find
  Fulfillment.
RACHEL.   What within my breast will then
  Replace it? It's forgotten how to swell
  Without a wish of wishes to command it.—
  Will there be nothing? I'm afraid! . . .
DAYA.   My wish
  Will take the place of that fulfilled one; mine.
  My wish to see, in Europe, you in hands   20
  More worthy of you.
RACHEL.   Wrong.—What makes this wish
  Your very own, prevents that it should ever

Be mine. What calls you is your fatherland:
Should mine not hold me? Should an image only
Of your beloved kin, which in your soul
Is not yet faded, have more weight with me
Than those I see, whom I can clasp and hear,
My people?

DAYA.   You may struggle as you will!
The ways of heaven are the ways of heaven.
And were it your deliverer himself   30
Through whom his God, for whom he fights, should
    lead
Your person to that distant folk for whom
You once were born!

RACHEL.   What are you saying, Daya,
What foolishness! Strange notions you do have!
"His God! for whom he fights!" Who can own
    God?
What God is that whom any man can own?
Who lets himself be fought for?—And how can
One know he's born *for* any spot on earth,
If not for that *on* which his birth took place?—
What if my father heard you!—How has he   40
Deserved that you should dream my happiness
As far away from him as possible?
And that the seeds of reason, which he sowed
So purely in my soul, you should now mix
With weeds or flowers from your native land?—
Beloved Daya, once for all, he will
Not see your pretty flowers on my soil.—
And I must tell you, that I feel my soil,
However fair they make it look, depleted,
Exhausted by your blossoms; feel myself   50
Amid their fragrance, faintly sour-sweet,

So giddy, so benumbed!—No doubt your brain
Is used to it. And so I do not chide
The stronger nerves which can endure it. But
It suits me not at all; and then your angel,
How close he came to making me a fool!—
I'm still ashamed, before my father, of
That farce!
DAYA.   What farce!—As if pure reason dwelt
  Nowhere but here!! Farce, farce! O, dared I speak!
RACHEL. Do you not dare? When was I not all ears,   60
  As often as you chose to pass the hours
  By telling of the heroes of your faith?
  Have I not always heard with admiration
  Their deeds, and wept at all their sufferings?
  It's true, their faith has never seemed to me
  Their most heroic trait. So much the more
  Consoling was their doctrine, that submission
  To God is wholly independent of
  Our notions about God.—My father, Daya,
  Has told us that so often; you yourself   70
  Have often thought him right: why undermine
  What you and he together have erected?—
  My Daya, this is not the kind of talk
  With which we best might meet our friend. For me
  It's helpful. For to me it is important
  Beyond all words to know if he . . . Hark, Daya!
  What is that at our door? If it were *he!*

SCENE 2

VOICE *(outside)*. Please walk in here! *(Enter Tem-*
  plar.)
RACHEL *(starts, composes herself, tries to fall at the*

Templar's feet).   It's he!—My savior, ah!

TEMPLAR. This to prevent I have delayed: and yet—

RACHEL. If I would clasp the feet of this proud man,
It's but to thank our God and not the man.
He wants no thanks, as little as the bucket
Which showed such zeal in putting out the fire,
Which let itself be filled and emptied, quite
Indifferent: just so the man. He too
Was simply thrust into the fire, and so
By chance, I fell into his arms, and stayed   10
By chance, as might a spark upon his cloak;
Until I don't know what had cast us both
Out of the flames again.—What cause is there
For thanks?—Mere wine in Europe has impelled
To greater deeds by far.—And Templar knights
Are duty-bound to act so; must indeed,
Like dogs of somewhat better training, fetch
From fire as well as water.

TEMPLAR *(Observing her with astonishment and dis-
      quiet).*   Daya, Daya!
If I had spells of bitterness and grief,
And took them out on you, why let her know   20
Each word of folly that escaped my tongue?
That was revenge beyond a proper measure!
I only hope henceforth you'll plead my cause
More kindly with her.

DAYA.   I should hardly think
The tiny stabs which you have dealt her heart
Have harmed you there.

RACHEL.   You say you suffered grief?
And were more stingy with that grief than with
Your life itself?

TEMPLAR.   My good and gracious child!—
   How is my spirit rent twixt eye and ear!—
   Not *this* girl was it, no, not she indeed,   30
   Whom from the fire I fetched.—Who could know
      her,
   And not do as I did? Who then had waited
   For me to come?—Still—fear—distorted looks—
   (Pause, as he loses himself in contemplation of her.)
RACHEL. But as for me, I find you still the same.—
   *(Pause continued; until she resumes talking, in order
      to break in upon his gazing.)*
   Well, Templar, tell us, do, where have you been
   So long?—Almost I might inquire as well:
   Where are you now?
TEMPLAR.   I am—where I perhaps
   Ought not to be.—
RACHEL.   Where you have been?—And where
   You think perhaps you ought not to have been?
   That is not good.   40
TEMPLAR.   At—at—what is the name?
   At Sinai.
RACHEL.   You have been at Sinai?—Good!
   Then I may surely learn reliably
   If it is true . . .
TEMPLAR.   What? what? If it is true
   That there the spot is to be seen, where Moses
   Stood before God, when . . .
RACHEL.   That is not the point.
   He stood 'fore God wherever he stood. Of that
   I know as much as I require.—No, what
   I'd like to learn from you is this: they say
   It's far less toilsome to ascend that mount

Than to descend it.—Every time I climbed   50
A mountain, it was just the opposite.—
Well, Templar?—What?—You turn away from me?
Look not at me?

TEMPLAR.   Because I want to hear you.

RACHEL. Because you would not let me see that you
Smile at my simpleness; yes, that you smile
To find I have no weightier thing to ask
About this holiest of all holy hills?
Is that it?

TEMPLAR.   Then into your eyes I must
Gaze once again.—And now you cast them down?
Repress your smile? just when I'd like to read   60
In doubtful looks what I so plainly hear,
What you so audibly confess—you're mute?—
Ah, Rachel, Rachel! Justly did he say,
"Wait till you know her!"

RACHEL.   Who?—Of whom?—Who
said it?

TEMPLAR. "Wait till you know her!" so your father
said,
To me, of you.

DAYA.   Did I not say it too?
Not I as well?

TEMPLAR.   But speak, where is he now?
Where is your father? Is he with the Sultan?

RACHEL. Beyond a doubt.

TEMPLAR.   Still there?—Forgetful me!
No, no, he'd not stay there so long.—I think   70
He's waiting for me by the cloister there;
Quite certainly; I think we so agreed.
Allow me! I will go to fetch him . . .

DAYA.   That
  Is mine to do. Stay, Templar, stay. I'll bring
  Him here without delay.

TEMPLAR.   Not so, not so!
  It is myself he wants to meet; not you.
  Besides, how easily he might . . . who knows? . . .
  With Saladin, you see, he might . . . you know
  The Sultan not! . . . he might have got into
  Embarrassment.—Believe me: there is danger   80
  Unless I go.

RACHEL.   How so? what sort of danger?

TEMPLAR. Danger for me, for you, for him: unless
  I swiftly, swiftly go. *(Exit.)*

SCENE 3

RACHEL.   What is this, Daya?
  So quickly?—What befell him? What new notion
  Impels him?

DAYA.   Never mind. I think it is
  A not unhopeful sign.

RACHEL.   A sign? Of what?

DAYA. That something stirs within him. Now it boils,
  Must not boil over. Let him be. Now it's
  Your turn.

RACHEL.   My turn for what? Like him, you grow
  Incomprehensible.

DAYA.   Quite soon you can
  Repay him all the unrest that he made
  You suffer. But be not too hard on him,   10
  Too greedy for revenge.

RACHEL.   What you are saying,

I hope you know yourself.

DAYA.   Well then, are you
Again so tranquil now?

RACHEL.   Yes. Yes, I am . . .

DAYA. At least confess you're glad of his disquiet;
And that to this you owe the mood of peace
You now enjoy.

RACHEL.   Of that I am aware!
For what at most I might confess to you
Is that I am myself amazed to find
How on a raging tempest in my heart
A calm like this could straightway thus ensue.   20
The sight of him, his speech, his actions have . . .

DAYA. Brought surfeit to you?

RACHEL.   Surfeit's not the word;
No—far from that.—

DAYA.   Assuaged the pangs of hunger.

RACHEL. Well, you might call it so.

DAYA.   Not I, indeed.

RACHEL. He'll be for ever dear to me, yes, dearer
Than my own life; what though my pulse no more
Is altered by his very name; my heart
No longer, when I think of him, will throb
More strongly, faster.—Why this prattle? Come,
Come, Daya, once more join me at the window   30
Which looks toward the palms.

DAYA.   And so I think
They are not quite assuaged, your hunger's pangs.

RACHEL. And now again I shall be seeing palms:
Not only him beneath the palms.

DAYA.   This coldness
No doubt begins another fever-spell.

RACHEL. How so? I am not cold. In truth, I see
   With no less pleasure what I see with calm.

SCENE 4

(Saladin, Sittah. Audience chamber in the palace of Saladin.)

SALADIN *(as he enters, speaks toward the door)*. Bring
   the Jew here, as soon as he arrives.
   (To Sittah.) He does not seem to hurry overmuch.
SITTAH. No doubt he was not right at hand; and not
   So quickly found.
SALADIN.   Ah, sister, sister!
SITTAH.   My,
   You take this like a battle.
SALADIN.   True, and one
   With arms I have not learned to wield. Shall I
   Dissemble; stir up apprehensions; set
   A trap or two; lure on to slippery ground?
   When did I so? Where could I learn the like?—
   And all this I must do, for what? For what?—   10
   To fish for money; money!—Yes, to scare
   Mere money from a Jew! And am I brought
   At last to stoop to such insipid wiles
   To gain the pettiest trifle of them all?
SITTAH. The smallest trifle, overly contemned,
   Will have its vengeance, brother.
SALADIN.   All too true.—
   And now what if this Jew should prove to be
   The good and wise one, as the Dervish once
   Described the man to you?

SITTAH.   Oh, in that case!
No need for worry. For the snare is set   20
To catch the stingy, fearsome Jew, the man
Of wily ways, but not the good and wise.
For such a Jew is ours without the snare.
The joy of hearing how he'll find excuse;
With what bold strength he'll either break the rope,
Or else with sly precautions writhe his way
Right past your nets; that you'll enjoy besides.
SALADIN. Well, that is true. Of course; I'm looking for-
    ward
To that.
SITTAH.   What else then can embarrass you?
For if it's merely one of many; if   30
He's merely Jew, as Jew: in sight of him
You will not be ashamed so to appear
As he thinks all men are? What's more, the man
Who shows a better face is but to him
A fool, a dupe.
SALADIN.   And so I must do evil,
Lest evil men think evil of my good?
SITTAH. Yes, brother, if you call it doing evil
To use each thing according to its kind.
SALADIN. What could a woman's brain invent, it could
Not also palliate!   40
SITTAH.   What, palliate!
SALADIN. I only fear, this dainty, subtle thing
Will crumble in my clumsy hand!—Such schemes
Must be performed precisely as invented:
With every skill and slyness.—Still, what odds!
I dance as best I can; though to be sure
I'd rather do it worse than better.
SITTAH.   Come,

Have confidence! For you I will go bail.
If you but will.—How prone are men like you
To make us think it was their sword alone,
Their mighty sword had carried them so far.   50
The lion is ashamed, it's true, when he
Hunts with the fox:—of foxes, not of guile.

SALADIN. And that you women like to drag us men
Down to your level!—Leave me, go!—I think
I know my lesson.

SITTAH.   What? I am to go?

SALADIN. You had not meant to stay?

SITTAH.   Well, if not that . . .
In sight of you—still, in this ante-room—

SALADIN. To listen there? Nor that, my sister, if
I may insist.—Away! I hear the curtain;
He comes!—Beware of lingering! I'll keep watch. 60
(*As she withdraws, Nathan enters by another door;
Saladin has seated himself.*)

SCENE 5

SALADIN. Come nearer, Jew!—Still nearer!—Close to
me!—
And have no fear!

NATHAN.   That's for your foe to feel!

SALADIN. You say you're Nathan?

NATHAN.   Yes.

SALADIN.   Wise Nathan?

NATHAN.   No.

SALADIN. If you don't say it, yet the people do.

NATHAN. May be; the people!

SALADIN.   Yet you don't suppose
That I am scornful of the people's voice?—

I long have had a wish to know the man
Whom they call wise.

NATHAN.   And if it were in scorn
They called him so? If to the people 'wise'
Were nothing more than 'shrewd'? and shrewd were
   he   10
Who knew his interest well?

SALADIN.   Of course you mean
His genuine interest?

NATHAN.   Why then indeed
Most selfish were most shrewd. And shrewd and
   wise
Were one.

SALADIN.   I hear you prove what you'd deny.—
Mankind's true interests, to the folk unknown,
Are known to you; at least you've tried to know
   them;
You've pondered them; and that alone produces
The wise man.

NATHAN.   As each thinker thinks he is.

SALADIN. Enough of modesty! For when one longs
To hear dry reason, constant modesty   20
Is sickening. *(He jumps up.)* Let's come to business,
   Jew.
But with sincerity!

NATHAN.   Your Highness, I
Will surely serve you so that I shall seem
Well worth your custom.

SALADIN.   Serve me? what?

NATHAN.   You shall
Obtain the best in all things; have it, too,
At lowest rates.

SALADIN.   What do you mean? I hope

It's not your wares?—I'll let my sister haggle
And bargain with you. *(Aside.)* That's for listening
  ears!
(Aloud.) With you as merchant I have no concern.
NATHAN.   Then doubtless you will wish to know
  what I   30
Have met or noted on my way about
The foe, who is indeed astir again? If I
May plainly speak . . .
SALADIN.   That too is not the goal
  I'm steering for with you. Of that I know
  All that I need.—In short . . .
NATHAN.   Command me, Sultan.
SALADIN. I seek instruction from you now in quite
  A different field.—Since you're accounted wise:
  Then tell me, pray—what faith, or moral law,
  Has most appeal for you?
NATHAN.   Your Highness knows
  I am a Jew.   40
SALADIN.   And I a Mussulman.
  The Christian stands between us.—Of these three
  Religions only one can be the true one.—
  A man like you does not remain where chance
  Of birth has cast him: if he so remains,
  It's out of insight, reasons, better choice.
  Well, then! such insight I would share with you.
  Let me the reasons know, which I have had
  No time to ponder out. Reveal to me
  The choice determined by these reasons plain—
  Of course in confidence—that I as well   50
  May make your choice my own.—This startles you?
  You weigh me with your eye?—It may well be
  No other Sultan has had such caprice;

Although I think it not unworthy quite
Of any Sultan.—Am I right?—Then speak!—
Speak out!—Or would you have a moment's time
To think it over? Good; I'll grant you that.—
(Aside.) Has she been listening? I will go and see;
I'll ask if she approves of me. *(Aloud.)* Reflect!
Reflect, make haste! For I shall soon return.   60
(He goes into the ante-room into which Sittah with-
drew.)

SCENE 6

NATHAN. H'm! h'm!—how strange!—I'm all confused.
  —What would
  The Sultan have of me?—I thought of money;
  And he wants—truth. Yes, truth! And wants it so—
  So bare and blank—as if the truth were coin!—
  And were it coin, which anciently was weighed!—
  That might be done! But coin from modern mints,
  Which but the stamp creates, which you but count
  Upon the counter—truth is not like that!
  As one puts money in his purse, just so
  One puts truth in his head? Which here is Jew?   10
  Which, I or he?—But stay!—Suppose in truth
  He did not ask for truth!—I must admit,
  Suspicion that he used the truth as trap
  Would be too small by far.—Too small?—What is
  Too small for one so great? — That's right, that's
    right:
  He rushed into the house incontinent!
  One knocks, one listens, surely, when one comes
  As friend.—I must tread warily!—But how?—
  To be a Jew outright won't do at all.—

But not to be a Jew will do still less. 20
For if no Jew, he might well ask, then why
Not Mussulman?—That's it! And that can save me!
Not only children can be quieted
With fables.—See, he comes. Well, let him come!

SCENE 7

SALADIN *(returning, aside)*. There, now the coast is
  clear!—*(Aloud.)* I hope I come
  Not prematurely?—You are at an end
  With your deliberations.—Well then, speak!
  No soul will hear us.
NATHAN.   Let the whole world listen.
SALADIN. So sure is Nathan of his case? Now there
  Is wisdom! Not to hide the truth! To stake
  One's all upon it! Life and limb! One's goods
  And blood!
NATHAN.   Yes, when it's needful and of use.
SALADIN. Henceforth I may expect to hold by rights
  One of my names, Reformer of the world   10
  And of the law.
NATHAN.   Indeed, a handsome title!
  But, Sultan, ere I draw the final veil,
  Allow me, please, to tell an ancient story.
SALADIN. Why not? I always was a friend of tales
  Well told.
NATHAN.   To tell them *well* is not, I fear,
  My forte.
SALADIN.   Proud modesty again?—Tell on!
NATHAN. In days of yore, there dwelt in eastern lands
  A man who had a ring of priceless worth
  Received from hands beloved. The stone it held,

An opal, shed a hundred colors fair,   20
And had the magic power that he who wore it,
Trusting its strength, was loved of God and men.
No wonder therefore that this eastern man
Would never cease to wear it; and took pains
To keep it in his household for all time.
He left the ring to that one of his sons
He loved the best; providing that in turn
That son bequeath to his most favorite son
The ring; and thus, regardless of his birth,
The dearest son, by virtue of the ring,   30
Should be the head, the prince of all his house.—
You follow, Sultan.

SALADIN.   Perfectly. Continue!

NATHAN. At last this ring, passed on from son to son,
Descended to a father of three sons;
All three of whom were duly dutiful,
All three of whom in consequence he needs
Must love alike. But yet from time to time,
Now this, now that one, now the third—as each
Might be with him alone, the other two
Not sharing then his overflowing heart—   40
Seemed worthiest of the ring; and so to each
He promised it, in pious frailty.
This lasted while it might.—Then came the time
For dying, and the loving father finds
Himself embarrassed. It's a grief to him
To wound two of his sons, who have relied
Upon his word.—What's to be done?—He sends
In secret to a jeweler, of whom
He orders two more rings, in pattern like
His own, and bids him spare nor cost nor toil   50
To make them in all points identical.

The jeweler succeeds. And when he brings
The rings to him, the sire himself cannot
Distinguish them from the original.
In glee and joy he calls his sons to him,
Each by himself, confers on him his blessing—
His ring as well—and dies.—You hear me, Sultan?

SALADIN *(who, taken aback, has turned away).* I hear,
I hear you!—Finish now your fable
Without delay.—I'm waiting!

NATHAN.   I am done.
For what ensues is wholly obvious.—   60
Scarce is the father dead when all three sons
Appear, each with his ring, and each would be
The reigning prince. They seek the facts, they quar-
    rel,
Accuse. In vain; the genuine ring was not
Demonstrable;—*(he pauses for a reply)*
                almost as little as
Today the genuine faith.

SALADIN.   You mean this as
The answer to my question? . . .

NATHAN.   What I mean
Is merely an excuse, if I decline
Precisely to distinguish those three rings
Which with intent the father ordered made   70
That sharpest eyes might not distinguish them.

SALADIN. The rings!—Don't trifle with me!—I should
    think
That those religions which I named to you
Might be distinguished readily enough.
Down to their clothing; down to food and drink!

NATHAN. In all respects except their basic grounds.—
Are they not grounded all in history,

Or writ or handed down?—But history
Must be accepted wholly upon faith—
Not so?—Well then, whose faith are we least like 80
To doubt? Our people's, surely? Those whose blood
We share? the ones who from our childhood gave
Us proofs of love? who never duped us, but
When it was for our good to be deceived?—
How can I trust my fathers less than you
Trust yours? Or turn about.—Can I demand
That to your forebears you should give the lie
That mine be not gainsaid? Or turn about.
The same holds true of Christians. Am I right?—
SALADIN *(aside)*. By Allah, yes! The man is right. I
    must   90
Be still.
NATHAN. Let's come back to our rings once more.
As we have said: the sons preferred complaint;
And each swore to the judge, he had received
The ring directly from his father's hand.—
As was the truth!—And long before had had
His father's promise, one day to enjoy
The privilege of the ring.—No less than truth!—
His father, each asserted, could not have
Been false to him; and sooner than suspect
This thing of him, of such a loving father: 100
He must accuse his brothers—howsoever
Inclined in other things to think the best
Of them—of some false play; and he the traitors
Would promptly ferret out; would take revenge.
SALADIN. And then, the judge?—I am all ears to hear
What you will have the judge decide. Speak on!
NATHAN. Thus said the judge: unless you swiftly bring
Your father here to me, I'll bid you leave

My judgment seat. Think you that I am here
For solving riddles? Would you wait, perhaps,   110
Until the genuine ring should rise and speak?—
But stop! I hear the genuine ring enjoys
The magic power to make its wearer loved,
Beloved of God and men. That must decide!
For spurious rings can surely not do that!—
Whom then do two of you love most? Quick, speak!
You're mute? The rings' effect is only backward,
Not outward? Each one loves himself the most?—
O then you are, all three, deceived deceivers!
Your rings are false, all three. The genuine ring   120
No doubt got lost. To hide the grievous loss,
To make it good, the father caused three rings
To serve for one.

SALADIN.   O splendid, splendid!

NATHAN.   So,
The judge went on, if you'll not have my counsel,
Instead of verdict, go! My counsel is:
Accept the matter wholly as it stands.
If each one from his father has his ring,
Then let each one believe his ring to be
The true one.—Possibly the father wished
To tolerate no longer in his house   130
The tyranny of just one ring!—And know:
That you, all three, he loved; and loved alike;
Since two of you he'd not humiliate
To favor one.—Well then! Let each aspire
To emulate his father's unbeguiled,
Unprejudiced affection! Let each strive
To match the rest in bringing to the fore
The magic of the opal in his ring!
Assist that power with all humility,

With benefaction, hearty peacefulness,   140
And with profound submission to God's will!
And when the magic powers of the stones
Reveal themselves in children's children's children:
I bid you, in a thousand thousand years,
To stand again before this seat. For then
A wiser man than I will sit as judge
Upon this bench, and speak. Depart!—So said
The modest judge.

SALADIN.   God! God!

NATHAN.   Now, Saladin,
If you would claim to be that wiser man,
The promised one . . .   150

SALADIN *(rushing to him and seizing his hand, which he*
            retains)   I, dust? I, nothing? God!

NATHAN. What is the matter, Saladin?

SALADIN.   Dear Nathan!—
The thousand thousand years your judge assigned
Are not yet up.—His judgment seat is not
For me.—Go!—Go!—But be my friend.

NATHAN.   Nought else
Had Saladin to tell me?

SALADIN.   Nought.

NATHAN.   Nought?

SALADIN.   Nothing.—
Why ask?

NATHAN.   May I seek opportunity
To ask a favor?

SALADIN.   And for that you need
An opportunity?—Speak out!

NATHAN.   I have returned
From distant parts, where I collected debts.—
I've almost too much cash on hand.—The times   160

Are once more looking doubtful;—and I know
Not rightly where to find security.—
I wondered, then, if you perhaps—because
Prospective war needs money more and more—
Could use some.

SALADIN *(looking him fixedly in the eye).* Nathan!—
    I'll not ask you if
Al-Hafi has been with you;—nor explore
If some suspicion urges you to make
This voluntary offer . . .

NATHAN.   A suspicion?

SALADIN. I'd be to blame.—Forgive me!—What's the
    use?
I must confess to you—I was indeed   170
Intending—

NATHAN.   Surely not, the selfsame thing
To ask of me?

SALADIN.   Quite so.

NATHAN.   Then both of us
Are helped at once!—But that I cannot send
All of my cash to you, ascribe that to
The youthful Templar.—One well known to you.—
To him I first must pay a goodly sum.

SALADIN. A Templar? Surely you would not support
My fiercest foes with means of yours?

NATHAN.   I speak
But of the one whose life you spared . . .

SALADIN.   Ah! that
Reminds me!—I had quite forgot the youth!—   180
Where is he? Do you know him?

NATHAN.   What? Then you
Are not aware, how much of what you gave
To him in mercy flowed through him to me?

For, risking all his newly granted life,
He saved my daughter from the fire.
SALADIN.   He did?—
　　Ha! So he looked, I thought. My brother would
　　Have done the same, whom he so much resembles.—
　　Is he still here? Then bring him to me!—For
　　I've told my sister of her brother, whom
　　She never knew, so many things that I   190
　　Must have her see his living image too!—
　　Go, fetch him!—Strange, how out of *one* good deed,
　　Though but a child of passion, such a wealth
　　Of other goodly deeds is born. Go, fetch him!
NATHAN *(dropping Saladin's hand)*. At once! And
　　　　our agreement stays in force? *(Exit.)*
SALADIN. Too bad I did not let my sister listen!—
　　To her!—How shall I tell her all of this?
　　(Exit at the other side.)

SCENE 8

(Under the palms in the vicinity of the monastery; the Templar is waiting for Nathan.)

TEMPLAR *(struggling with himself, walks up and down; then he bursts out)*.—The wearied victim
　　　　pauses here.—What then!
　　I *will* not know just what goes on in me;
　　Nor yet anticipate what is to be.—
　　Enough to say, I fled in vain! in vain.—
　　Yet all I *could* was flee!—Now come what must!—
　　Too swift the blow for me to dodge its fall;
　　Although to shun it I so oft, so much,
　　Had used refusal.—Seeing her, whom I

So little craved to see—yes, seeing her
Meant the resolve to let her nevermore   10
Escape my sight—Resolve, how so? Resolve
Is purpose, action; and I merely suffered.
To see her and to feel myself enmeshed,
One texture with her being, was the same;
Remains the same.—To live apart from her
Is quite unthinkable; that would mean death—
And wheresoever after death we bide,
There too my death.—If that is love, why then—
The Templar loves indeed—the Christian loves
The Jewish maid indeed.—Well! What of that?—
In this the Land of Promise—hence to me   21
Of Promise likewise to eternity!—
I've rid myself of many a prejudice.—
What would my Order have? As Templar, I
Am dead; was from that moment dead to it,
Which made me prisoner to Saladin.
That head which he gave back, was it my own?—
No, it's a new one, ignorant of all
That was impressed on that one, bound it fast.—
And better, too, for my paternal heaven   30
More suitable. I feel that now. With it
I now begin to think as in these lands
My father must have thought; unless it's fables
They've told me of him.—Fables?—only quite
Believable; more credible, indeed,
They never seemed than now, when I but run
The risk of stumbling where he fell.—He fell?
I'd rather fall with men than stand with children—
His model guarantees me his applause.
Is there another whose applause I crave?   40
Nathan's, I wonder?—His encouragement,

Beyond applause, can hardly fail me less.—
Ha, what a Jew!—And one who likes to seem
Just Jew, no more!—He comes, and comes with
    haste;
Aglow with joy. But who comes otherwise
From Saladin?—Ho, Nathan!

SCENE 9

NATHAN *(entering).*   Is it you?
TEMPLAR. You tarried very long with Saladin.
NATHAN. Oh, not so long. I was too much delayed
    In getting there.—Yes, truly, Curt; the man
    Matches his fame. His fame is but his shadow.—
    But first of all let me report to you . . .
TEMPLAR. What then?
NATHAN.   He wants to see you; bids you come
    To him without delay. Escort me home,
    Where I have things to order for his service.
    Then we will go to him.   10
TEMPLAR.   Your dwelling, Nathan,
    I'll enter not again, until . . .
NATHAN.   Then you
    Have been there meanwhile? seen and spoken to
        her?—
    Well?—Tell me; how does Rachel please you?
TEMPLAR.   Oh,
    Beyond all words!—And yet—I never will—
    Consent to see her more! Unless right here
    You promise me that I may see her face—
    For ever.
NATHAN.   How should I interpret that?
TEMPLAR *(after a short pause, falling on his neck).*
    My father!

NATHAN.   Well, young man!

TEMPLAR *(releasing him just as suddenly)*. Not son?
—I beg you!—

NATHAN. My dear young man!

TEMPLAR.   Not son?—I beg you, Nathan!—
    Conjure you by the foremost bonds of nature!— 20
    Give not precedence to much later ties!—
    Suffice it just to be a man!—And thrust
    Me not from you!

NATHAN.   My dear, dear friend! . . .

TEMPLAR.   And son?
    Not son?—Not even then, if gratitude
    Had guided love to your dear daughter's heart?
    Not even then, if both but wait your nod
    To fuse and melt in one?—You say no word?

NATHAN. You have surprised me, knight.

TEMPLAR.   You are surprised?—
    Surprise you, Nathan, with your very thoughts?
    You'd not disown them, spoken by my lips?— 30
    And I surprise you?

NATHAN.   Till I know for sure
    Which Stauffen was your father!

TEMPLAR.   Nathan, not—
    At such a time, instead of feelings warm,
    You're curious?

NATHAN.   For look you, I myself
    Once knew a Stauffen, and his name was Conrad.

TEMPLAR. And what if my own father bore that name?

NATHAN. Truly?

TEMPLAR.   I bear my father's name: for Curt
    Is Conrad.

NATHAN.   Well—my Conrad then was not
    Your father. For my Conrad was like you:

A Templar; never married.   40
TEMPLAR.   All the same!
NATHAN. What?
TEMPLAR.   All the same he might quite well have
    been
    My father.
NATHAN.   You are jesting.
TEMPLAR.   And in truth
    You're too pedantic!—For what were I now?
    Granted, a by-blow or a bastard! Still
    The stock is not to be despised at that.—
    But give me leave to blink my pedigree,
    I'll do as much by you. Not that I have
    The slightest doubt of your descent. No, God
    Forbid! You trace it, shoot by shoot, clear back
    To Abraham. And backward from there on   50
    I know it too; will take my oath on it.
NATHAN. You're growing bitter.—Do I merit that?—
    Have I refused you?—No, I merely would
    Not take you at your word this very moment.—
    It's nothing more.
TEMPLAR.   For sure?—And nothing more?
    O, then forgive . . .
NATHAN.   Come quickly, come!
TEMPLAR.   Where to?
    No!—With you to your house?—Not that, not
        that!—
    There's fire there!—I'll await you here. Begone!—
    If ever I see her more I'll see her then
    Often enough. If not, then I have seen   60
    Her far too much . . .
NATHAN.   I'll hasten as I can. (*Exit.*)

SCENE 10

TEMPLAR. More than enough!—The human brain can
  grasp
  So boundlessly; yet on a sudden is
  Sometimes so full! and of a trifle full!—
  No use, no use; and let it be surcharged
  With what it will.—Let me have patience now!
  The soul will take the turgid stuff and blend
  It soon in one, thus gaining space, and light
  And order will return.—Say, is this love
  The first I've known?—Or was what I have known
  As love not love?—Is love none other than   10
  I'm feeling now? . . .
DAYA *(who has stolen in from the side).* Sir Knight!
  Sir Knight!
TEMPLAR.   Who calls?
  Well, Daya, you?
DAYA.   I've stolen past him. But
  He still could see us, where you stand.—So come
  Closer to me, behind this tree.
TEMPLAR.   What now?
  Such secrecy? What is it?
DAYA.   Ah, indeed
  It is a secret that impels me to
  Your side; a double secret. One is known
  To me alone; the other known to you.—
  Suppose we trade; your secret tell to me,
  Then I will tell you mine.   20
TEMPLAR.   With pleasure.—If
  You'll tell me first what you consider mine.
  But that no doubt your secret will make clear.—

So you begin.
DAYA.   Imagine!—No, sir Knight:
  First you; I'll follow.—Be assured that mine
  Is nothing worth to you, unless I've yours
  Before.—Make haste!—For if I question you:
  You have confided nothing. Then my secret
  Remains my own; and you are rid of yours.—
  Alas, poor knight!—To think you men believe
  You *could* have a secret from our sex!   30
TEMPLAR. Often a secret we don't know we have.
DAYA. May be. And so indeed I must be kind
  Enough to give yourself the information.—
  What did it mean that to your heels you took
  So suddenly? and left us in the lurch?—
  And why don't you return with Nathan now?—
  Did Rachel have such slight effect on you?
  Or else, so much?—It *was* so much!—Teach me
  To know the fluttering of the captured bird,
  Stuck to the lime!—In short: confess at once   40
  You love her, love her close to madness; and
  I'll tell you something . . .
TEMPLAR.   Madness? Truly; you
  Are quite a judge of that.
DAYA.   Well, just admit
  The love at least; I'll let the madness go.
TEMPLAR. Because it's obvious?—A Templar knight
  Should love a Jewess! . . .
DAYA.   Granted, that appears
  To make but little sense.—And yet at times
  There's more sense in a thing than we suspect;
  Would it be so amazing, if the Saviour
  Should draw us to him by such ways as shrewd-
      ness   50

Would not be like to choose?
TEMPLAR.   Such solemn tone?—
  (Aside.) But if I think of Providence instead
  Of Christ, is she not right?—*(Aloud.)* I grant, you
    make
  Me curious as I'm seldom wont to be.
DAYA. This is the land of wonders!
TEMPLAR *(aside)*.   Well!—let's say
  Of wondrous things. Can it be otherwise?
  The whole world comes together here.—*(Aloud.)*
    Dear Daya,
  Assume as granted what you'd have me say:
  That I do love her; that I fail to see
  How I shall live without her; that indeed . . .   60
DAYA. Truly, sir Knight?—Then swear to make her
    yours;
  To save her; yes, to save her here on earth,
  Eternally in heaven.
TEMPLAR.   How?—How can I?—
  How can I swear what's not within my power?
DAYA. It is within your power. And with a word.
  A single word, I'll put it in your power.
TEMPLAR. That even her father would have no
    objection?
DAYA. Her father! stuff! He'll *have* to give consent.
TEMPLAR. Will *have* to, Daya?—Up to now he's not
  In robber's hands.—There's nothing that he *must*
    do.
DAYA. Well then, he must agree; and willingly.   71
TEMPLAR. Must, willingly!—But if I tell you, Daya,
  I've tried myself to touch this chord in him?
DAYA. And he did not respond in harmony?
TEMPLAR. No, in *disharmony*, which—wounded me.

DAYA. What say you?—What? You showed him but
    a shadow
  Of a desire for Rachel, and he failed
  To leap for joy?—he frostily withdrew,
  Made difficulties?
TEMPLAR.   Just about.
DAYA.   Then I
  Will hesitate no longer—*(Pause.)*   80
TEMPLAR.   Yet I see
  You hesitate?
DAYA.   He is so good a man!—
  I owe him much myself.—To think that he
  Should stop his ears!—God knows, with bleeding
    heart
  I put such pressure on him
TEMPLAR.   Daya, please
  Free me at once from this uncertainty.
  But if you are yourself unsure, if what
  You have in mind should good or bad be called,
  Shameful or laudable—then hold your peace!
  I will forget you've something to conceal.
DAYA. That spurs instead of checking. Well; then
    learn;   90
  Rachel is not a Jewess; is—a Christian.
TEMPLAR *(coldly)*. Congratulations! Was the birthing
    hard?
  Don't mind the labor pains!—Go on
  With zeal to people heaven; now that you
  Can add no more to earth.
DAYA.   What, knight? Deserves
  My news such scorn? That Rachel is a Christian:
  That gladdens you, a Christian and a Templar,
  Who love her well, no more?

TEMPLAR.   Tremendously,
  Since she's a Christian of your special brand.
DAYA. So that's your thought? Let it be so!—But no!
  I'd like to see the one who should convert her! [100]
  Her fortune is, long since to be what she
  Has lost the power to become.
TEMPLAR.   Explain
  Or—go!
DAYA.   She is a Christian; born of Christians;
  And is baptized . . .
TEMPLAR. (*hastily*). And Nathan?
DAYA.   Not her father!
TEMPLAR. He's not her father?—Know you what you
    say?
DAYA. The truth, which often cost me bitter tears.—
  No, he is not her father . . .
TEMPLAR.   As his daughter
  He reared her only? Reared this Christian child
  As Jewess for himself?
DAYA.   Quite so.
TEMPLAR.   Not knowing
  How she was born?—She never learned from
    him   110
  That she was born a Christian, not a Jewess?
DAYA. No, never!
TEMPLAR.   Did not merely rear the *child*
  In this delusion? Left the girl as well
  Thus uninformed?
DAYA.   Too true!
TEMPLAR.   Thus acted—Nathan?
  This wise, good Nathan should have been so free
  To falsify the voice of nature thus?—
  Thus to misguide the impulse of a heart

Which, left alone, would take quite other ways?—
You have indeed confided to me, Daya,   120
A thing of weight—which may have conse-
    quences—
Perplexes me—puts me in present doubt
What I should do.—So give me time!—And go!
He'll pass this place again. He might surprise us.
So go!

DAYA. O, that would kill me!

TEMPLAR.   I am quite
Unfit to see him now. If you should meet him,
Just tell him that again we'll come together
At Saladin's.

DAYA.   But let him not suspect
A thing.—This should but give to the affair
A final shove; should free you of all doubts   130
Regarding Rachel!—If you take her then
To Europe, surely, me you will not leave
Behind?

TEMPLAR. That's to be seen. But go now, go. *(Both go
    out, Daya first.)*

ACT IV

SCENE 1

(The cloisters of the monastery.)

FRIAR. Yes, yes! no doubt the Patriarch is right!
   Although so far I've not had much success
   With what he's bid me do.—Why put on me
   Just tasks like those?—I hate this subtlety;
   I hate persuasion; hate to stick my nose
   In everything; and hate to have my hands
   In everything.—Did I forsake the world,
   Myself alone, to get myself entangled
   With worldly things? For others all the more?
TEMPLAR. *(hurrying up to him)*. Good brother!
   There you are. I long have sought you.   10
FRIAR. Me, sir?
TEMPLAR.   Have you forgotten me so soon?
FRIAR. Oh no! I only thought that in my life
   Never again I'd get to see your face.
   Such was my prayer to God.—The dear God knows
   How bitter to me was the mission which
   I was obliged to lay before you; knows
   If I desired to find an open ear
   In you; and knows how greatly I rejoiced,
   With all my heart, that you so bluntly brushed 19
   Away from you, without much thought, all that
   Which does not grace a knight.—Yet you return;
   The seed has taken root.
TEMPLAR.   You know, it seems,
   Why I have come? I scarcely know myself.

FRIAR. You've thought it through, and found, the
    Patriarch
    Is not so very wrong; that gold and honor
    His project might secure to you; and that
    A foe's a foe, and were he seven times
    Our angel. This you've weighed with flesh and blood,
    And come and will agree to serve.—Oh dear!
TEMPLAR. My good and pious man! be comforted   30
    It's not for that I come, . . . and would consult
    The Patriarch. As yet upon that point
    I think as then I thought; not for the world
    Would forfeit now the good opinion which
    An honest, dear, and pious man like you
    Once held of me.—I merely come to ask
    The Patriarch's advice upon a thing . . .
FRIAR. You ask the Patriarch? A knight a—*priest?*
    (*Looking around fearfully.*)
TEMPLAR. The thing is rather priestly.
FRIAR.   All the same,
    The priest won't ask the knight, and were the thing
    All knightliness.   41
TEMPLAR.   Because he has the right
    To make mistakes; which I am not inclined
    To envy him.—Of course, if I had but
    To act here for myself; of course, if I
    Had but to answer to myself; what need
    Had I of Patriarchs? But certain things
    I'd rather settle by another's will
    And badly, than quite well by mine alone.—
    Besides, as now I see, religion is
    Party as well; and one may think he is   50
    Unpartisan, yet find that willy-nilly
    He waves his party's flag. Since that is so,

It's doubtless right.

FRIAR.   On that I'll make no comment,
Not sure I understand my lord.

TEMPLAR.   And yet!—
(*Aside.*) Let's see, what do I really want? Decree,
Or counsel?—Simple-hearted, or refined?—
(*Aloud.*) I thank you, brother, for the friendly
    hint.—
Why Patriarch?—Be you my Patriarch!
For in the Patriarch it's more the Christian
Whom I would ask, than the other way around.— 60
The case is this . . .

FRIAR.   No further, sir, no further!
What use?—You do misjudge me.—He who knows
Too many things has many cares; and I
Have vowed myself to *one* alone.—Oh, good!
Hark! look! There comes, to my relief, himself.
Remain right here. He has caught sight of you.

SCENE 2

(*The Patriarch approaches through one of the cloisters
in full priestly regalia.*)

TEMPLAR. I wish that I could shun him.—Not my
    taste—
A red-faced, fat, and all too friendly prelate!
And what display!

FRIAR.   You ought to see him dressed
To go to court. But now he's only been
Sick-visiting.

TEMPLAR.   How Saladin will pale
Before him!

PATRIARCH (*approaching, motions to the Friar.*)
                    Here!—No doubt that is the Templar.

What does he want?

FRIAR.   Don't know.

PATRIARCH *(approaching him, as the Friar and retinue
    withdraw.)*   Well, knight!—Delighted
    To see this fine young man!—Well, still so young!
    With God's aid, something can be made of you.

TEMPLAR. But scarcely more, Your Worship, than you
        see.   10
    And rather less, I think.

PATRIARCH.   At least I hope
    That such a pious knight for years may bloom
    And flourish for the benefit and honor
    Of Christendom and God's beloved cause!
    Nor can this fail to be, if bravery
    Of youth be guided by the mellowed counsel
    Of age.—How else might I to you be helpful?

TEMPLAR. With that which youth like mine oft sadly
        lacks:
    Advice.

PATRIARCH. Right willingly!—Yet the advice
    Must be obeyed.   20

TEMPLAR.   Not blindly?

PATRIARCH.   Who says that?
    No one, of course, must fail to use the reason
    Which God has given him—where it belongs.—
    But is that everywhere?—O no!—For instance:
    If God should deign through his own angel's lips—
    That is to say, a servant of His word—
    To let us know a means whereby the weal
    Of Christendom, the health of holy Church,
    In any quite especial way can be
    Advanced or strengthened: who may then presume
    With reason to explore the will of Him   30

Who has created reason, and to test
The everlasting law of heaven's glory
By petty rules of vain and earthly honor?—
Enough of this.—What is it then, sir Knight,
On which for now you would have our advice?

TEMPLAR. Supposing, reverend Father, that a Jew
Possessed an only child—call it a girl—
Whom with the greatest care in all things good
He had brought up, and loved more than his soul,
And who most piously returned his love.   40
And now we were informed, the child was not
The Jew's own daughter: he had picked it up
In childhood, bought or stolen—what you will;
The girl was known to be a Christian child,
Baptized; the Jew had merely reared her as a Jewess;
And caused her to remain as Jewess and
His daughter:—tell me, Father, in such case
What should one do?

PATRIARCH.   I shudder!—First, however,
My Lord should state if such a case is fact
Or mere hypothesis. That is to say: 50
If he has but imagined this, or if
It has occurred, and so continues.

TEMPLAR.   I
Believed that was all one, if I but wished
Your Worship's judgment.

PATRIARCH.   One? I pray you, mark
How our proud human intellect can err
In churchly things.—By no means! If the case
Presented is but pastime of the mind:
Would it be worth the toil to think it through
In earnest? Then I'd urge my Lord to try
The theatre, where such things *pro et contra*   60

Could be discussed with general applause.—
But if you do not play some trick on me
With a theatric prank; and if the case
Is fact; and should it even have transpired
Within this diocese Jerusalem,
Our well-beloved city:—then, indeed—

TEMPLAR. What then, pray?

PATRIARCH.   First of all, upon the Jew
The punishment must be inflicted, which
Imperial and papal law decree
For such a villainous and vicious crime.

TEMPLAR. It must?

PATRIARCH.   And the aforesaid laws impose
Upon the Jew who to apostasy   70
Seduce a Christian soul—the funeral pyre,
The stake—

TEMPLAR.   They do?

PATRIARCH.   And how much more the Jew
Who forcibly a helpless Christian child
Withdraws from his baptism bond? For is
Not all that's done to children done by force?—
That is:—excepting what the church to them
May do.

TEMPLAR. But if the child, had not the Jew
Had pity on it, had perhaps succumbed
To misery?

PATRIARCH.   All one! The Jew must burn.
For better if it died in misery   80
Than that for its damnation everlasting
It thus were saved.—Besides, why should the Jew
Forestall the Lord? Whom God would save, He can
Preserve without him.

TEMPLAR.   Or despite the Jew

Make blessed, I should think.
PATRIARCH.   All one! The Jew
  Must burn.
TEMPLAR.   I find that hard! The more that he,
  So people say, has reared the girl not in
  His faith, but rather in no faith at all,
  And taught this child not more or less of God
  Than reason would require.   90
PATRIARCH.   All one! The Jew
  Must burn . . . Yes, for this cause alone deserves
  To burn threefold!—What? let a child grow up
  With no belief at all?—The solemn duty
  Of faith to leave unmentioned to a child?
  O, that is vile!—And I'm surprised, sir Knight,
  That you . . .
TEMPLAR.   The rest, Your Worship, if God will,
  When I confess. *(Starts off.)*
PATRIARCH.   What? fail a full account
  To render me?—This criminal, this Jew,
  Not name to me?—not fetch him here to me?—
  But I know what to do! I'll go at once   100
  To Saladin!—By the capitulation
  His oath confirmed he *must* protect our rights;
  In all the laws protect us, all the dogmas,
  Which we account a part of our most holy
  Religion! We have the original,
  Thank God! We have his hand and seal. Yes, *we!*—
  And easily I'll make him see what danger
  Lies for the state itself in lack of faith.
  All civic bonds dissolved and rent asunder,
  When men need not believe.—Away! away   110
  With such a crime! . . .
TEMPLAR.   Too bad I can't enjoy

This splendid sermon with more leisure time!
For Saladin has sent for me.
PATRIARCH.   He has?
    Well then—Of course—Why then—
TEMPLAR.   I will prepare
    The Sultan, if Your Worship so desire.
PATRIARCH. Oh, oh!—I know that you have found
    much favor
    With Saladin!—I beg you will report
    But good of me to him.—It's only zeal
    For God that does impel me. If I err
    In overdoing, it's for Him.—I pray   120
    You'll bear that fact in mind!—And then, sir knight,
    The matter of the Jew you have brought up
    Was just a problem?—that's to say, was just—
TEMPLAR. A problem. *(Exit.)*
PATRIARCH *(to himself)*. Which however I must seek
    To ferret out. That might be just the task
    For Brother Bonafides. *(Aloud.)* Here, my son!
    (He talks to the Friar while going off.)

SCENE 3

*(A room in the palace of Saladin, into which a quantity
of bags are being carried by slaves and placed side by
side on the floor.)*

SALADIN *(entering)*. Upon my word! not ended yet.
    —Is there
    Much more of this to come?
A SLAVE.   The half, I think.
SALADIN. Then take the rest to Sittah.—Now where is
    Al-Hafi? Let Al-Hafi take this over

At once.—Or should I send it out to Father?
All trickles through my fingers, here.—Although
One does grow hard at last; and surely now
It takes some skill to get much out of me.
Until at least the moneys due from Egypt
Are here, let poverty make shift and try 10
To get along!—If at the Sepulchre
Alms do not cease; if but with empty hands
The Christian pilgrims need not go from hence!
If but—

SITTAH *(enters)*. What is all this? What means the gold
You've sent?

SALADIN.   Repay yourself with it; and stow
Away for futures what remains.

SITTAH.   Is Nathan
Not here yet with the Templar?

SALADIN.   No, he seeks
Him everywhere.

SITTAH.   Just see what I have found
The while my ancient jewelry passed through
My hands. *(Showing him a small painting.)* 20

SALADIN.   My brother, ha!—It's he, it's he!—
Or it was he, alas!—Dear, doughty lad,
That you I lost so young! What could I not
Have undertaken with you at my side!—
Give me the picture, Sittah. I recall
It well: he gave it to your older sister,
His Lilla, who one morning simply would
Not let him leave her arms. It was the last,
His final ride.—And I had let him ride
And ride alone!—Ah, Lilla died of grief,
Never forgave me that I let him go 30
All by himself.—He came no more.

SITTAH.   Poor brother!

SALADIN. Oh well!—One day we all will come no
   more!—
   Besides—who knows? It is not only death
   Which for a youth like him may shift the goal.
   Such youths have other foes; the strongest one
   May yield him to the weakest.—Well, be that
   As may.—I must compare the picture with
   The youthful Templar; must assure myself
   How much my fancy has deceived me.

SITTAH.   Yes,

   For that alone I brought it. But return   40
   It, give it back! On this I must insist:
   A woman's eye is best at that.

SALADIN *(to a door-keeper who enters).* Now who
   Is there?—the Templar?—Bid him come!

SITTAH.   That I
   Disturb you not, with curiosity
   Confuse him not—*(She seats herself on a sofa at one
      side and drops her veil.)*

SALADIN.   Ah, good!—*(Aside.)* And now his
   voice!
   How will it sound!—I think that Assad's tone
   Must still be sleeping somewhere in my soul!

SCENE 4

TEMPLAR *(enters).* It's I, your captive, Sultan . . .

SALADIN.   What, my captive?
   Whom I present with life, do I not give
   Him freedom too?

TEMPLAR.   That which is meet for you
   To do, is meet for me to hear, but not

Anticipate. But, Sultan—to accord
You special thanks for life restored is not
In keeping with my character and rank.—
In any case once more it's at your service.
SALADIN. Employ it not against me!—I admit
An extra pair of hands I'd not begrudge   10
My enemy. But such a heart as well,
That I'd regret.—I'm not a whit deceived
In you, my noble youth! I find you are
My Assad, soul and body. See! I could
Inquire where you have been these many years?
What cavern held your sleep? What fairyland,
What kindly elf has kept this flower fresh
From year to year? I could remind you, too,
Of what we did together, there or there.
Or I could chide you, that *one* secret you   20
Did keep from me, and *one* adventure hid!—
Yes, that I could; if I but looked at you,
Not at myself as well.—Well, be it so!
Of this sweet revery so much is true,
That in my autumn Assad once again
Shall bloom for me.—With your consent, young
    knight?
TEMPLAR. Whatever comes to me from you—and be
It what it may—that lay as wish within
My soul.
SALADIN. Of this let us at once make trial.—
Would you remain with me? Here at my side?— 30
As Christian, Mussulman, all one! In cloak
Of white, in Moslem robe; in turban, or
In Christian cowl: just as you will. All one!
I never have required the selfsame bark
To grow on every tree.

TEMPLAR.   Or else I think
    You'd not be what you are: the hero, who
    Had rather be God's gardener.
SALADIN.   Then: if you
    Have no worse thought of me than this, we are
    Already half agreed?
TEMPLAR.   No, quite!
SALADIN *(giving him his hand)*. A word?
TEMPLAR *(taking his hand)*. A man! Herewith   40
    receive far more than you
    Could take from me. Forever yours!
SALADIN.   Too much
    Of gain for just one day! too much!—Did he
    Not come with you?
TEMPLAR.   Who?
SALADIN.   Nathan.
TEMPLAR *(frostily)*.   No. I came
    Alone.
SALADIN. What noble deed was yours? And what
    A wise provision, that a deed so fine
    Should benefit a man so noble.
TEMPLAR.   Oh.
SALADIN. So cold?—No, no, young man! If God
    through us
    Does something good, we must not be so cold!
    Nor modesty make us appear so cold!
TEMPLAR. To think that every thing in this our
    world   50
    Should have so many sides!—Of which, quite often,
    One can't imagine how they fit together!
SALADIN. Hold always to the best, and honor God!
    He knows just how they fit together.—But
    If you must be so difficult, young man,

No doubt I too must needs be on my guard
With you? For I too am a thing, alas!
Of many sides, which often seem to fit
Each other ill.

TEMPLAR.   That hurts!—Suspicion is
No common fault of mine—   60

SALADIN.   Well, tell me, then,
Of whom you feel it?—Seemingly, of Nathan.
Are you suspecting Nathan? You?—Explain!
Come, give me this first proof of confidence.

TEMPLAR. Against him I have nothing. I'm just angry
With my own self.—

SALADIN.   At what?

TEMPLAR.   Because I dreamed
A Jew might once forget to be a Jew;
And dreamed with open eyes.

SALADIN.   Then out with it,
This waking dream!

TEMPLAR.   You know of Nathan's daughter.
The thing I did for her I did because—
I did it. Then, too proud to harvest thanks   70
Where I'd not sown it, day by day I scorned
To see the girl again. The father was
Away; he comes, he hears; he seeks me out;
He thanks me; wishes that his daughter may
Appeal to me; he speaks of prospects, speaks
Of hope and cheer.—And so I find myself
Persuaded, go there, look, and find in truth
A maiden . . . Sultan, I am so ashamed!—

SALADIN. Ashamed?—Because on you a Jewish girl
Made an impression? No, don't tell me that!   80

TEMPLAR. Because my hasty heart, persuaded by
The father's prattle, made so weak a stand

Gainst that impression!—Fool! a second time
I leaped into the fire.—For now I sued,
And *I* was scorned.

SALADIN.   You, scorned?

TEMPLAR.   The father wisely
Does not refuse me outright. But he first
Must make inquiry, must reflect. Of course!
Did I not do the same? Did I not make
Inquiry first, reflect, when in the fire
She shrieked?—In truth! God, it's a pretty thing, 90
To be so wise, so cautious!

SALADIN.   Come now, come!
Be not so hard on age! And then, how long
Can his refusals last? Will he demand
Of you that you become a Jew?

TEMPLAR.   Who knows?

SALADIN. Who knows?—the one who knows what
    Nathan is.

TEMPLAR. The superstition in which we grew up,
    Though we may recognize it, does not lose
    Its power over us.—Not all are free
    Who make mock of their chains.

SALADIN.   A sage remark!
But Nathan truly, he . . .   100

TEMPLAR.   That superstition
Is worst which takes itself to be of all
The most endurable . . .

SALADIN.   That may well be!
But Nathan . . .

TEMPLAR.   And to which alone one may
Entrust dull-witted humankind, till it's
Accustomed to the brighter light of truth.

SALADIN. All right! But Nathan!—Nathan's destiny
  Is not such weakness.
TEMPLAR.   So I too believed! . . .
  But if this paragon of men were such
  A common Jew that he would try to gain
  Control of Christian children, that he might   110
  Rear them as Jews:—what then?
SALADIN.   Who tells such tales
  Of him?
TEMPLAR. The very girl with whom he would
  Decoy me, with the hope of whom he'd like
  To seem to pay me for the service which
  He would not take for nothing;—she is not
  His daughter; is a Christian child astray.
SALADIN. Whom none the less he would not give to
    you?
TEMPLAR (vehemently). Would or would not! He is
    unmasked. And thus
  The tolerant babbler is unmasked! I shall
  Contrive to set upon this Jewish wolf   120
  In philosophic sheepskin hounds whose teeth
  Shall tear his fleece!
SALADIN (seriously). Be quiet, Christian!
TEMPLAR.   What?
  Be quiet, Christian?—Now if Jew insists
  On Jew, and Mussulman on Mussulman:
  Shall only Christians be forbid to act
  The Christian?
SALADIN (more earnestly). Quiet, Christian!
TEMPLAR (calmly).   Yes, in full
  I feel the weight of the reproach—which you
  Compress into that word! Ah, if I knew

How Assad would have acted in this case!

SALADIN. Not greatly better!—Doubtless, quite as
    heady!—   130
    But who so soon has taught you, just like him,
    To bribe me with one word? It's true, if all
    The facts are as you state them, I myself
    In them cannot find Nathan.—Yet he is
    My friend, and of my friends not one may quarrel
    With others!—Be advised! Go cautiously!
    Nor give him up at once into the hands
    Of your fanatic rabble! Don't reveal
    The things your clergy, for revenge on him,
    Would challenge me to do!—In narrowness   140
    Don't emulate or Jew or Mussulman
    In being Christian!

TEMPLAR.   If not yet too late,
    That's due the Patriarch's bloodthirstiness,
    Whose tool I shuddered to become!

SALADIN.   What's that?
    You sought the Patriarch's advice before
    My own?

TEMPLAR. In passion's tempest, in the whirl
    Of indecision!—Pardon!—Ah, I fear
    You will no longer wish to see in me
    Your Assad's likeness.

SALADIN.   Had you not expressed
    This very fear! I think I know the faults   150
    From whence our virtue sprouts. But nurture *this*,
    And *they* shall scarcely harm you in my eyes.—
    But go!—Seek Nathan, as he sought for you;
    And bring him here. For I must reconcile
    You two.—And if in earnest you desire
    The maiden: be at rest. She shall be yours!

And Nathan too shall feel it, that he dared
To rear a Christian without pork!—Now go!
(*Exit Templar; Sittah quits the sofa.*)

SCENE 5

SITTAH. How strange!
SALADIN.   You feel it, Sittah? Must my Assad
   Not have been handsome, and a fine young man?
SITTAH. If so he was, and not for just this picture
   The Templar sat!—But how could you forget
   To ask about his parents?
SALADIN.   I suppose
   Especially his mother? Whether she
   Had ever seen this land?
SITTAH.   You make me smile!
SALADIN. Nothing more possible! For Assad was
   To pretty Christian ladies always welcome,
   On pretty Christian ladies so intent,   10
   That once they even said—Oh well, one speaks
   Reluctantly of that.—Enough: I have
   Him back!—and will with all his faults, with all
   The whimsies of his tender heart, be glad
   To have him back!—O! Nathan must bestow
   The girl on him. What think you?
SITTAH.   What, bestow?
   Surrender!
SALADIN.   To be sure! What sort of claim
   Has Nathan to her, since he's not her father?
   Who thus has saved her life, he only holds
   The rights of him who gave her life.   20
SITTAH.   Suppose,
   My Saladin, you brought her straightway here?

Withdrawing her straightway from the unrightful
Possessor?
SALADIN.   Is that needful?
SITTAH.   Needful, no!—
It's curiosity alone impels me
To give you this advice. With certain men
I greatly like to know as soon as may be
What sort of girl attracts them.
SALADIN.   Well, then send
And have her brought.
SITTAH.   Oh, may I, brother?
SALADIN.   But
Consider Nathan! Nathan must not think
That we would take the girl from him by force.   30
SITTAH. Be not afraid of that.
SALADIN.   And I must see
Where my Al-Hafi is.

SCENE 6

*(The open vestibule in Nathan's house, looking toward
the palms; as in Act I, Scene 1.—A part of the wares
and jewels lie unpacked.)*

DAYA.   O, all is splendid!
All choice! O, all—as only you can give it.
Where, where is made this silver stuff with sprigs
Of gold? What does it cost?—That's what I call
A bridal dress! No queen could ask for better.
NATHAN. A bridal dress? Why only that?
DAYA.   Oh well!
Of course you did not think of that when you

Were buying it.—But truly, Nathan, this
And this alone is it! As if you'd picked
It out as wedding dress. The background white, 10
Denoting innocence; the golden streams
Which everywhere meander through the ground,
Denoting wealth. You see? Enrapturing!

NATHAN. Why all this show of wit? Whose bridal
dress
You symbolize so learnedly?—Are you
Betrothed?

DAYA.   I?

NATHAN.   Who, then?

DAYA.   I — good God!

NATHAN.   Then who?
Whose wedding dress are you describing here?—
These things belong to you, and no one else.

DAYA. To me? And meant for me?—And not for
Rachel?

NATHAN. What I have brought for Rachel, that is
packed   20
In quite another bale. Quick! take it hence!
Pick up your stuff and go!

DAYA.   You tempter, you!
No, no, and even if it were the jewels
Of all the world! I touch them not, unless
You swear to me to take advantage of
This opportunity, the like of which
Heaven won't send you twice.

NATHAN.   Advantage? what?—
And opportunity? for what?

DAYA.   O act
Not so obtuse!—In brief: the Templar loves

Our Rachel: give her to him! Then your sin,   30
Which I no longer can conceal, will have
An end; the girl will thus return to Christians;
Once more be what she is; and is once more
What she became; and you, with all the good
For which we cannot give you thanks enough,
Will not have merely heaped up coals of fire
Upon your head.

NATHAN.   Ah ha, the same old harp?—
Just strung with one new string, which, I'm afraid,
Cannot be tuned nor made to hold.

DAYA.   How so?

NATHAN. The Templar would be fine with me. I'd give
Him Rachel sooner than to any other.   41
But yet . . . Have patience.

DAYA.   Patience? Is that not
Your ancient harp?

NATHAN.   A few more days of patience! . . .
Look, look!—Who comes this way? A brother friar?
Go, ask him what he wants.

DAYA.   What should he want?
(She goes to question him.)

NATHAN. Then give!—before he asks.—*(Aside.)* If I
but knew
How I could first accost the Templar, yet
Not tell the reason for my curious quest!
For if I tell him, and what I suspect
Is groundless: then in vain I've placed at stake   50
My interest as a father.—*(To Daya.)* Well, what
now?

DAYA. He wants to speak with you.

NATHAN.   Then let him come;
And go the while.

SCENE 7

(Nathan and the Lay Brother.)

NATHAN *(aside)*.   How gladly I'd remain
As Rachel's father!—Can't I *be* so still,
Though I should lose the name?—Indeed, with her
I'll keep the name as well, if once she knows
How much I crave it. *(To Daya.)*—Go! *(Exit
Daya.) (To the friar.)* How can I serve
Your need, good brother?

FRIAR.   I've but little need.—
I'm happy, Nathan, still to see you well.

NATHAN. You know me, then?

FRIAR.   Why, sir, who knows you not?
You have impressed your name on many a hand.
The impress is on mine, these many years.   10

NATHAN *(reaching for his purse)*.
Come, brother, I'll refresh the print.

FRIAR.   No, thanks!
I'd steal it from the needy; I'll take nothing.—
But if you will permit me, I'll refresh
My name with you. For I've the right to boast
Of laying something in *your* hand, and not
Contemptible.

NATHAN.   Forgive!—I am ashamed—
Remind me!—take as penance sevenfold
The value of it from me now.

FRIAR.   But first
Be told how I myself this very day
Was minded of the pledge entrusted you.   20

NATHAN. A pledge entrusted me?

FRIAR.   Not long ago

I sat as hermit, near to Jericho,
On Quarantana.* Arab robbers came,
Broke down my chapel and my cell, and dragged
Me off with them. But I escaped, with luck,
And journeyed hither to the Patriarch,
To beg of him another spot, where I
In solitude might serve my God unto
My blessed end.
NATHAN.   I stand on coals, good brother.
  Be brief. The pledge! The pledge entrusted me!   30
FRIAR. One moment, Nathan.—Well, the Patriarch
  Assured me of a hermitage on Tabor,**
  So soon as one was free; but meantime bade
  Me stay as friar in the cloister here.
  There I am serving, Nathan; wish myself
  A hundred times a day on Tabor. For
  The Patriarch employs me for such things
  As fill me with great loathing. For example:
NATHAN. Make haste, I beg you!
FRIAR.   Well, it's coming now!
  Today somebody whispered in his ear:
  That hereabouts there lives a Jew who has
  A Christian child brought up as his own daughter.
NATHAN *(Startled)*. What's this?
FRIAR.   Just hear me to the end.—The while
  He orders me to trace this Jew at once,
  If possible, and he is most enraged
  At such offense, which seems to him to be

---

  * A desert land between Jericho and Jerusalem, where Christ
is said to have spent the forty days (hence the name) of his
temptation; a high, rugged mountain still bears the same name.
  ** Mount Tabor, six miles southeast of Nazareth.

The very sin against the Holy Ghost;—
That is, the sin, which of all sins we count
The greatest sin, but that we, God be praised,
Don't rightly know in what that sin consists;—   50
At once my conscience wakes; and it occurs
To me that I myself, in times gone by,
Might well have given opportunity
For this unpardonable sin.—I ask you,
Did not a horseman, eighteen years ago,
Bring you a baby girl, a few weeks old?
NATHAN. How so?—Well, yes—that's true—
FRIAR.   Come, look at me
Right sharply!—For that horseman, that was I.
NATHAN. Was you?
FRIAR.   The lord, from whom I brought it, was,
If I am right—a Lord von Filnek—Wolf   60
Von Filnek.
NATHAN.   Right!
FRIAR.   Because its mother had
But lately died; and since the father was
Dispatched—I think to Gaza *—suddenly,
To where the infant could not follow him:
He sent it you. And as I think I found you
In Darun? **
NATHAN.   Right again!
FRIAR.   I would not wonder,
If memory deceived me. I have had
So many goodly masters; and this one
I served but all too briefly. Very soon

* A fortified seaport which Saladin attacked and took in 1170.
** Built not long before by a king of Jerusalem on a height
near Gaza.

He fell at Ascalon; * I think he was   70
  A gallant gentleman.
NATHAN.   He was! he was!
  To whom I owe so much, so much of thanks!
  Who more than once had saved me from the sword!
FRIAR. How fine! So much the gladder were you then
  To take his little daughter.
NATHAN.   That you can
  Imagine well.
FRIAR.   Well then, where is it now?
  I surely hope the daughter has not died?—
  O better let it not have died!—And if
  Nobody knows of the affair: then all
  Is well.   80
NATHAN.   Is well?
FRIAR.   Have trust in me. For see,
  I think this way: if on the Good, which I
  Believe I'm doing, something very bad
  Too closely borders: then I'll rather not
  Perform the Good; because the Bad we know
  Reliably enough, but we are far
  From knowing what is good.—How natural,
  That if that Christian baby should be reared
  Most properly, you'd bring it up as yours.—
  And this you should have done in love and faith,
  And must get such reward? I can't see that.   90
  Admittedly, it had been shrewder if
  You'd had the Christian by another hand
  Brought up as Christian: in that case you'd not

---

  * Also named Ashkelon, a fortified seaport captured by
Baldwin III in 1153, retaken by Saladin in 1187 and demolished
in 1191.

Have loved the daughter of your friend. And chil-
　　dren
Have need of love—and were it but the love
Of savage beasts—much more than Christian teach-
　　ing.
For Christianity there's always time.
If but the girl before your eyes has grown
In health and soulfulness, in Heaven's eyes
She still is what she was. Is it not true   100
That Christendom is built on Jewish faith?
I've oft been angered, moved to bitter tears,
When Christians could so utterly forget
That our Lord Jesus was a Jew himself.

NATHAN. Good brother, you must be my advocate,
If hatred and hypocrisy should rise
Against me—for an act—Ah, for an act!
You only shall be told of it!—But take
It with you to the grave! Mere vanity
Has never tempted me as yet to tell it   110
To any other. You alone I'll tell it.
To simple piety alone I'll tell it.
Since that alone can understand the deeds
God-fearing man can force himself to do.

FRIAR. I see you moved, your eyes are filled with tears?

NATHAN. At Darun you had found me with the child.
But you will hardly know that just before
In Gath * the Christians slaughtered all the Jews
With wives and children; know not, that among
These Jews my wife with seven hopeful sons   120
Was domiciled within my brother's house,

* One of the five royal cities of Philistia, northwest of Jerusalem.

Sent to him for safekeeping, where they all
Were burned to death.

FRIAR.   O righteous God!

NATHAN.   And when
You came, three days and nights I had been lying
In dust and ashes, weeping unto God.—
Weeping? Far more: with God had argued, stormed,
Enraged, and cursed myself and all the world;
And sworn against the Christian world a hate
Irreconcilable —

FRIAR.   I well believe it!

NATHAN. But bit by bit my reason found return.   130
With gentle voice it spoke: "And yet God is!
That too was God's decree! Up then, and come!
Now practice what you long have understood;
And what is scarcely harder to perform
Than just to comprehend, if you but will.
Arise!"—I stood and cried to God: I will!
If Thou wilt, then I will!—Then you dismounted
And handed me the child, wrapped in your cloak.—
What you then said to me; or I to you:
I have forgotten. Only this I know: 140
I took the child, I bore it to my couch,
I kissed it, threw myself upon my knees,
And sobbed: O God! for seven *one* at least!

FRIAR. O Nathan, Nathan! You're a Christian soul!
By God, a better Christian never lived!

NATHAN. And well for us! For what makes me for you
A Christian, makes yourself for me a Jew!—
But let's no longer melt each other's hearts.
Here deeds are needed. And though sevenfold love
Soon bound me to this single waif and girl;   150
Though in the thought I perish, that anew

I am to lose my seven sons in her:
If Providence demands her at my hands
Again—I shall obey!
FRIAR.   See there!—So much
I had myself been ready to advise you!
And now your guardian angel has already
So counseled you!
NATHAN.   But still, the first chance claimant
Must not abduct her!
FRIAR.   Surely not!
NATHAN.   Or one
Who had not greater rights to her than I;
At least he must have prior ones—   160
FRIAR.   Of course!
NATHAN. Which blood and nature grant him.
FRIAR.   Just my thought!
NATHAN. So quickly name the man who's kin to her
As brother, uncle, cousin, or the like:
I will not then withhold her, who was born
And reared to be of any faith and house
The ornament.—I hope that of your lord
And of his race you know much more than I.
FRIAR. Alas, good Nathan, hardly that.—You have
Already heard that all too brief a time
I was with him.   170
NATHAN.   Do you not know at least
The mother's family?—Was she a Stauffen?
FRIAR. Quite possible!—I think so.
NATHAN.   Was her brother
Not named Conrad von Stauffen—and a Templar?
FRIAR. Unless I err. But stop! It comes to me
That I possess from my lamented lord
A little book. I drew it from his breast

At Ascalon, when we interred him.
NATHAN.   Well?
FRIAR. It's full of prayers. We call it breviary.—
    A Christian, so I thought, might have a use
    For that.—Not I, indeed.—I cannot read—   180
NATHAN. No matter.—To the point!
FRIAR.   Well, in this book
    At front and back, as I've been told, and in
    My lord's own hand, are fully written down
    His relatives and hers.
NATHAN.   O welcome news!
    Go! run! fetch me the book! I shall be glad
    To pay its weight in gold; a thousand thanks
    Besides! Haste! run!
FRIAR.   Right gladly! But it is
    In Arabic, the writing of my lord. (*Exit.*)
NATHAN. All one! Just bring it!—God, if I could keep
    The maiden still, and purchase me besides   190
    A son-in-law like that!—I doubt it!—Well,
    Let be what may!—But who can it have been
    That let the Patriarch get wind of this?
    That I must not forget to ask.—What if
    It even came from Daya?

SCENE 8

DAYA (*in haste, embarrassed*). Nathan, fancy!
NATHAN. Well, what?
DAYA.   Poor child, she was in consternation!
    There sends . . .
NATHAN.   The Patriarch?
DAYA.   The Sultan's sister,
    The Princess Sittah . . .

NATHAN.   Not the Patriarch?

DAYA. No, Sittah!—Don't you hear?—The Princess
    Sittah
  Sends hither, has our Rachel fetched.

NATHAN.   Has whom?
  Our Rachel fetched?—And Sittah has her fetched?—
  Well; if it's Sittah has her fetched, and not
  The Patriarch . . .

DAYA.   Why should you think of him?

NATHAN. You've not heard anything from him of late?
  In truth? Nor whispered aught to him?   11

DAYA.   I, him?

NATHAN. Where are the messengers?

DAYA.   Outside.

NATHAN.   I will
  In caution's name accost them. Come!—If but
  There's nothing of the Patriarch in this. *(Exit.)*

DAYA. And I have quite a different fear. Let's see!
  The sole reputed daughter of a Jew
  So rich were for a Mussulman not quite
  Unmeet?—Then, flash! the Templar's out of luck.
  He is: unless I risk the second step;
  And to herself reveal just who she is!—   20
  Take heart! Let me employ the earliest moment,
  When I'm with her alone, for that.—Perhaps
  I'll use the very one when I escort her.
  A prior hint, while we are on our way,
  Can do no harm, at least. Yes, yes! That's it!
  It's now or never! On, and ever on! *(Follows*
    Nathan.)

ACT V

SCENE 1

(The room in Saladin's palace into which the money-bags had been carried; these can still be seen. Saladin and thereafter several Mamelukes.)

SALADIN *(entering)*. Here stands the money still; And no one knows
  Just where to find the Dervish, who, no doubt,
  Has stumbled on a chess-board, here or there,
  And so forgot himself;—then why not me?—
  Well, patience! *(To an entering Mameluke.)* Speak!
A MAMELUKE.   Most welcome tidings, Sultan!
  Rejoice, O Sultan! . . . See, the caravan
  From Cairo, long expected, has arrived,
  Is safe! with seven years of tribute from
  The prosperous Nile.
SALADIN.   Good tidings, Ibrahim!
  In truth, you are a welcome messenger!—   10
  At last it comes! at *last!*—Receive my thanks
  For goodly news.
MAMELUKE *(waiting; aside)*. Well, then! Let's have it!
SALADIN.   What is't
  You're waiting for?—Begone.
MAMELUKE.   And nothing more
  For my good news?
SALADIN.   What else?
MAMELUKE.   The messenger
  Of good gets nothing good?—Then I'm the first
  Whom Saladin has learned at last to pay
  With words!—That too is fame!—to be the first

122

With whom he played the niggard.

SALADIN.   Why then, take
  A money-bag.

MAMELUKE.   Not now I won't! In vain
  You'd offer all of them to me. *(He turns to go.)* 20

SALADIN.   This pride!—
  Come here! Here's two for you.—What, really
    going?
  Outdoes me in nobility?—For surely
  He must have found it harder to refuse
  Than I to give it him.—Ho, Ibrahim!—
  What urges me, so soon before my exit,
  To change my very nature all at once?—
  Will Saladin not die as Saladin?—
  For then as Saladin he should not live.

A SECOND MAMELUKE. Well, Sultan! . . .

SALADIN.   If you come to bring me news . . .

SECOND MAMELUKE. That now the train from Egypt
  has come in!   30

SALADIN. I know that.

SECOND MAMELUKE.   So I *was* too late!

SALADIN.   And why
  Too late?—So take of me for your good will
  A money bag or two.

SECOND MAMELUKE.   Why, that makes three!

SALADIN. Yes, if you're good at counting.—Take them,
  then.

SECOND MAMELUKE. I think a third will come as well—
  if he
  Succeeds in getting here.

SALADIN.   How so?

SECOND MAMELUKE.   Oh well;
  He's likely to have broke his neck! You see,

We three, so soon as we had certain news
The transport had arrived, each briskly sped
Away. The foremost fell; and so I took   40
The lead, and held it till we got to town;
Where Ibrahim, the rascal, knows by heart
The short-cuts.
SALADIN.   Pity on the fallen one!
    My friend, the fallen one!—Do ride to meet him.
SECOND MAMELUKE. Why, that I think I'll do!—And if
    he lives:
    The half of all this money shall be his. *(Exit.)*
SALADIN. Now what a good and noble knave is that!—
    Who else can boast of Mamelukes like these?
    And is it not permitted me to think
    That my example helped to mould them?—So,   50
    Have done with thinking that at journey's end
    I might accustom them to other ways! . . .
THIRD MAMELUKE. My Sultan, . . .
SALADIN.   Are you he that fell?
THIRD MAMELUKE.   Oh no,
    I come but to report that Emir Mansor,
    Who led the caravan, is now dismounting . . .
SALADIN. O bring him hither! quickly!—Here he is!
    (Enter Mansor.)

SCENE 2

(Saladin. Mansor.)

SALADIN. Be welcome, Emir! Well, how went your
    train?—
    O Mansor, long enough you made us wait!
MANSOR. This letter tells what tumults in Thebais *

* The country about Thebes in upper Egypt.

Your Abulkassem first was forced to quell,
Before we dared to set out on our way.
But then our march I did accelerate
As much as possible.
SALADIN.   That I believe!—
And take, good Mansor, take at once—I hope
You do it willingly?—fresh escort troops
At once. You must forthwith go on: you must   10
Convey the money's greater part at once
To Lebanon, to Father.
MANSOR.   Willingly!
SALADIN. And see to it your escort's not too weak.
At Lebanon it is no longer safe.
Have you not heard? The Templars are astir
Once more. So be upon your guard!—But come!
Where is the train? I'd like to see it; and
Take care of things myself.—(*To the servants.*)
    You there! Bring word
To Sittah I will join her presently.

SCENE 3

(*The palms before Nathan's house; the Templar walking up and down.*)

TEMPLAR. And once for all, his house I will not
    enter.—
He surely will appear again!—How soon,
How gladly they were wont to notice me!—
I should not wonder if he'd yet forbid
My frequent strolling here before his house.—
H'm!—I must say I'm very vexed.—And what
Embittered me so much against him?—For

He said, as yet he would refuse me nothing.
And Saladin has taken on the task
To win him over.—What? can it be true   10
The Christian in me sends down deeper roots
Than does the Jew in him?—Who knows him-
    self?—
Why else should I begrudge the little prey
He took such pains to capture for himself
Within the Christians' game-preserve?—Of course:
No paltry spoils, a creature such as that!
A creature? Whose?—No creature of the slave
Who floated to the desert shore of life
The shapeless block, and disappeared. Much more
The artist's, who in that abandoned block   20
Thought out the form divine which he portrayed.—
Ah! Rachel's sire in truth remains—despite
The Christian who begot her—now and ever
The Jew.—If I envision her as but
A Christian girl, bereft of all the traits
That only such a Jew could give to her:—
Speak, heart—what would she have to win your
    praise?
Nought! little! Even her smiling, were it nothing
But gentle, lovely twitching of her muscles;
Were that which makes her smile not worthy of   30
The charm in which it's clothed upon her lips:—
No, no; not even her smile! Far fairer smiles
I've seen misspent on folly, frippery,
On scoffing, flatterers, and paramours.—
Did they enchant me then? Did they bring out
In me the wish to flutter out my life
Beneath their sunshine?—Not that I recall.
And yet I'm out of sorts with him who gave,

And him alone, the higher worth she has?
How so? and why?—Do I deserve the gibe   40
With which the Sultan bade me go?—It's bad
Enough that Saladin could think it true!
How small he must have thought me then! and how
Contemptible!—And all that for a girl?—
Curt, Curt! this will not do. Change course! Suppose,
To cap all, Daya had but prattled something
Which could not well be proven.—See, at last
He comes, engrossed in conversation, from
His house!—Ah ha! with whom?—With him? My friar?—
Well! then he surely knows the whole! no doubt
Has been discovered to the Patriarch!—   51
What mischief have I in my folly done!—
See how one spark of passion can consume
So much intelligence!—Resolve at once
What now is to be done! I'll step aside
And wait; perhaps the Friar will depart.

SCENE 4

NATHAN *(as they approach)*. Again, good brother, many thanks!

FRIAR.   And you
As many!

NATHAN.   I? from you? For what? For my
Insistence in compelling you to take
What you don't need?—If your insistence had
Succumbed to mine; if you were not resolved
To be more rich than I.

FRIAR.   The book does not

Belong to me in any case; belongs
Much rather to your daughter; so to speak,
It is her sole paternal heritage.—
Oh well, she now has you.—May God but grant　10
That you may never need repent that you
Have done so much for her!

NATHAN.   Can I repent?
I never can. No fear of that!

FRIAR.   Well, well!
These Patriarchs and Templars . . .

NATHAN.   Have no power
To do me so much harm that anything
Could cause me to regret: that least of all!—
And are you then so very certain that
A Templar's egging on your Patriarch?

FRIAR. It scarce can be another. Such a knight
Had just had talk with him; and what I heard　20
Resembled this.

NATHAN.   And yet there is but one
Here in Jerusalem. And I know him;
He is my friend; a noble, frank young man!

FRIAR. Quite right; that's he!—But what one is, and
what
One must be in this world, that is not always
The same.

NATHAN.   Too true.—Let anyone who will,
Proceed to do his best or worst! For with
Your book, good brother, I'll defy them all;
And with it I'll go straight to Saladin.　29

FRIAR. Good luck! So then for now I'll leave you here.

NATHAN. And haven't even seen her?—Come again,
Come soon, and often.—On this day, I hope,
The Patriarch learns nothing yet!—But stay!

Tell him the truth if you desire.
FRIAR.   Not I.
  Farewell! *(Exit.)*
NATHAN.   And don't forget us, brother!—God!
  O that right here beneath the open sky
  I could fall on my knees! See how the knot
  Which often caused me fear unties itself!—
  O God! how light I feel, that now no more
  There's anything to hide in all the world!   40
  That I can walk so freely before men,
  As in Thy sight, O Thou who needest not
  To judge a man according to his deeds,
  The which indeed so seldom are his deeds!

SCENE 5

(Templar approaches Nathan from the side.)

TEMPLAR. Ho, Nathan, wait; take me along!
NATHAN.   Who calls?—
  It's you, sir knight? Where were you, when I
      thought
  To meet you at the Sultan's?
TEMPLAR.   We but missed
  Each other. Do not take offense!
NATHAN.   Not I;
  But Saladin . . .
TEMPLAR.   You had just gone . . .
NATHAN.   And so
  You saw him after all? Then all is well.
TEMPLAR. But he would have us come to him together.
NATHAN. So much the better. Come along. My course
  Was to him anyway.—

TEMPLAR.   May I inquire
Who left you there just now?   10
NATHAN.   Why, don't you know him?
TEMPLAR. Was it that good old soul, the Friar, whom
The Patriarch sends out to be a ferret?
NATHAN. May be! It's true he's with the Patriarch.
TEMPLAR. Not bad, that trick: to send the simple out
Before rascality.
NATHAN.   If stupid, yes;—
But not if pious.
TEMPLAR.   Which no Patriarch
Believes in.
NATHAN.   This is one I'll vouch for. He
Will never help his Patriarch in what
Is wicked.
TEMPLAR.   Such at least is his pretense.—
But has he said nothing to you of me?   20
NATHAN. Of you? No, not by name.—Indeed, he scarce
Can know your name.
TEMPLAR.   That's true.
NATHAN.   But of a Templar
He did say something . . .
TEMPLAR.   What?
NATHAN.   But you he could
Not possibly have meant!
TEMPLAR.   Who knows? Let's hear it.
NATHAN. That to his Patriarch one had accused me . . .
TEMPLAR. Accused you?—That is, by his leave—a
    lie.—
O hear me, Nathan!—I am not a man
Who's able to deny the truth. And what
I did, I did! But neither am I one
Who'd make defense of everything he did   30

As if well done. Why should I be ashamed
Of error? Have I not the best resolve
To better it? And don't I know, perhaps,
How far a man can get with such resolve?—
O hear me, Nathan!—Yes, I am the Templar
The Friar had in mind, who's said to have
Accused you.—Oh, you know what made me vexed,
What caused my blood to boil in every vein!—
I, imbecile!—I came, in soul and body
Prepared to throw myself into your arms.   40
How you received me—cold—lukewarm—the
    which
Is even worse than cold; how formally
You were at pains to seek evasions; how
With questions quite irrelevant you seemed
To wish to give me answer: even now
I scarce may think of this, if I would keep
Composure.—Hear me, Nathan!—Being in
This fermentation, Daya stole to me
And flung her secret in my face, which seemed
To me to hold the explanation of   50
Your dubious behavior.

NATHAN.   How?

TEMPLAR.   O let
Me finish!—I imagined that this child
Which you had shrewdly wrested from the
    Christians
You would be loath to yield to them again.
To make it short, I thought it would be good
To put the dagger at your throat.

NATHAN.   Hm, good?
Where is the good in that?

TEMPLAR.   O hear me, Nathan!—

It's true; I did a wrong!—And I presume
You are not guilty.—And that silly Daya
Knew not what she was saying—hates you, too— 60
And only wants to get you into trouble.—
May be, may be!—I'm just a stupid puppy,
Who tries to play both ends against the middle;
Does now too much, and now by far too little.—
That too may be. Forgive me, Nathan.

NATHAN.   If
    You come at me like that—

TEMPLAR.   In short, I sought
The Patriarch!—but mentioned not your name.
That's falsehood, I repeat! I merely placed
The case before him in a general way,
Asked his opinion.—Well, that too might well   70
Have stayed undone: of course!—Did I not know
The Patriarch as scoundrel? Could I not
Have questioned you at once?—Was I obliged
Thus to subject your daughter to the risk
Of losing such a father?—Well, what odds?
The prelate's villainy, which always stays
Consistent, brought me by the straightest path
Back to myself again.—For hear me, Nathan;
Just hear me out!—Suppose he knew your name:
What then, what then?—He cannot take the girl 80
From you unless she's no one's but your own.
And from *your* house he could but drag her to
The convent.—So—give her to me! Just give
The girl to me; and let him come. I think
He'll hardly dare to take my wife from me.—
Give her to me; and quickly!—Say she be
Your child, or not; be Christian, Jewess, neither!
All one, all one! I will not question you

About it, never, not in all my life.
No, be that as it may!   90
NATHAN.   You think I find
  It very needful to conceal the truth?
TEMPLAR. Well, be that as it may!
NATHAN.   I've not denied
  To you or those who'd have a right to know—
  That she's a Christian, only foster-daughter
  To me.—But why I've not to her revealed it?—
  I think that only calls for *her* forgiveness.
TEMPLAR. Which you'll not need of her.—Do her the
    favor
  That she may always see you as your child!
  And spare her this disclosure!—For as yet
  You only have control of her. But give   100
  Her life to me! I beg you, Nathan: do!
  It's I alone who for a second time
  Can rescue her—and will.
NATHAN.   Yes—could have, could have!
  No longer now. It is too late for that.
TEMPLAR. How so? too late!
NATHAN.   Thanks to the Patriarch . . .
TEMPLAR. The Patriarch? And thanks to him? What
    for?
  You mean *he* should have merited our thanks?
  For what, for what?
NATHAN.   That now we know to whom
  She is related; know into whose hands
  She can be safely laid.   110
TEMPLAR.   Let him give thanks
  For that who will have greater cause!
NATHAN.   From them
  You too must now receive her; not from mine.

TEMPLAR. Poor Rachel! Think of all you must endure,
  Poor Rachel! What for other orphans were
  A blessing turns to your misfortune.—Nathan!—
  Where are they now, these kinsfolk?
NATHAN.   Where they are?
TEMPLAR. And *who* are they?
NATHAN.   A brother specially
  Has come to light, to whom you'll have to sue
  For her.
TEMPLAR. A brother? What is he, this brother?
  A soldier? Or a churchman?—Let us hear   120
  What I may look for.
NATHAN.   Neither one, I think,—
  Or both at once. I know him not so well.
TEMPLAR. What else?
NATHAN.   A goodly man! In whom, I hope,
  Our Rachel will not be so badly off.
TEMPLAR. A Christian, though!—At times I cannot
    tell
  What I should think of you:—take no offense,
  Good Nathan!—Must she not the Christian play,
  Midst Christians? Not at last become what she
  Has now played long enough! Will not the weeds
  At last choke down the wheat you finely   130
    sowed?
  And that leaves you so calm? In spite of that,
  I hear you say yourself that with her brother
  She won't be badly off?
NATHAN.   I think and hope it!—
  And if with him there should be something lacking,
  Has she not you and me beside her?
TEMPLAR.   O!
  With him what should be lacking? Will he not

Provide his sister well with food and clothing,
With finery and sweetmeats plentiful?
What needs a sister more?—Oh yes, a man
Besides!—Oh well, him too in course of time   140
Will brother soon provide; he's easily found!
The Christianer the better!—Nathan, Nathan!
Think of the angel you had formed, whom now
Others will ruin!

NATHAN.   Have no fear! She will
Continue to prove worthy of our love.

TEMPLAR. Don't say that! Do not say it of *my* love!
For that will not be cheated, not of jot
Or tittle! nor of any name!—But stop!—
Does she suspect already what awaits her?

NATHAN. Perhaps; although I wouldn't know   150
from whom.

TEMPLAR. That too's all one; she shall in either case—
She must find out what fate has now in store
At first from me. My notion, not to see
Or speak to her again, till I should have
The right to call her mine, is void. I haste . . .

NATHAN. Where to?

TEMPLAR.   To her! To find out if her soul,
Though maidenly, has manhood in its veins
Enough to make the sole resolve which would
Be worthy her!

NATHAN.   Which one?

TEMPLAR.   This: not to pay
Much heed henceforth to you and to her   160
brother—

NATHAN. And?

TEMPLAR.   Follow me, regardless; even though
At last she should be married to a Moslem.

NATHAN. Remain! You will not find her. She's with
    Sittah,
    The Sultan's sister.
TEMPLAR.   What? Since when? and why?
NATHAN. And if you'd like to find the brother too
    There with them: come along.
TEMPLAR.   The brother? which?
    Sittah's or Rachel's?
NATHAN.   Both, perhaps. Come, come!
    (*Nathan leads him off.*)

SCENE 6

(*Sittah's harem.*)

SITTAH. Sweet girl, how glad I am to have you with
    me!—
    But don't be so uneasy, frightened, timid!—
    Be cheerful, talkative, and more familiar!
RACHEL. O Princess . . .
SITTAH.   No! not Princess! Call me
    Sittah—
    Your friend—your sister. Call me mother, too!—
    I could be that, you know.—So young, so wise,
    So good! The things you know! What must you
    not
    Have read!
RACHEL.   Have read?—O Sittah, you but mock
    Your silly little sister. Truly, I
    Can scarcely read.   10
SITTAH.   What, scarcely, little fibber!
RACHEL. My father's writing, some!—I thought you
    spoke

Of books.

SITTAH.   That's right! of books.

RACHEL.   Well, on my word
  I find books hard to read.

SITTAH.   You mean that?

RACHEL.   Yes,
  I do. My father loves, you see, too little
  That cold book-learning, which impresses on
  The mind just lifeless symbols.

SITTAH.   I'm surprised
  And yet he's not so wrong!—So what you
    know . . . ?

RACHEL. I only know from listening to him,
  And in most cases I could tell you still
  How, where, and why he taught it me.   20

SITTAH.   It's true,
  It's better then retained. And learning then
  Engrosses all the soul.

RACHEL.   I'm sure that Sittah
  Has likewise little or nothing read.

SITTAH.   How so?—
  I am not proud of it.—But still, how so?
  Your reason! Speak out boldly. What's your
    reason?

RACHEL. She is so simple; without artifice;
  Like no one but herself . . .

SITTAH.   And?

RACHEL.   Books will let
  Us seldom be like that: my father says.

SITTAH. O, what a man your father is!

RACHEL.   Oh yes!

SITTAH. How near he always seems to hit the   30
    mark!

RACHEL. Oh yes!—And now this father—
SITTAH.   Dear, what's wrong?
RACHEL. This father!
SITTAH.   What! You're weeping?
RACHEL.   Such a father—
   Ah! I must speak! My heart demands release . . .
   (She casts herself, overcome with weeping, at Sit-
   tah's feet.)
SITTAH. Dear child, what ails you? Rachel!
RACHEL.   I'm supposed—
   To lose this father!
SITTAH.   Lose him? *You* lose *him?*
   How so?—Be calm!—That shall not be!—Get up!
RACHEL. O, not in vain shall you have offered me
   To be my friend, my sister!
SITTAH.   Yes! I am!—
   Get up, get up! Or I must call for help.
RACHEL *(composing herself and getting up).*
   Pardon! forgive!—My pain made me forget   40
   What you are like. With Sittah no despair,
   No whimpering prevails. Cool, quiet reason
   Alone can plead successfully with her.
   Whose cause such reason pleads, he wins his case!
SITTAH. Well then?
RACHEL.   I know my friend and sister will
   Not suffer that! Will never suffer that
   Another father be imposed on me!
SITTAH. Another father? and on you imposed?
   Who can do that? or even want to, dear?
RACHEL. Who? It's my good, bad Daya that can want
   to—   50
   And claims she can.—Oh, yes, you do not know,
   I think, this good, bad Daya?—God forgive

Her this, I pray!—reward her, too! She has
Done me so much of good, so much of bad!
SITTAH. What, bad, to you?—Then, truly, she must
have
But little good in her.
RACHEL.   Oh, but she does,
Much good!
SITTAH.   Who is she?
RACHEL.   She's a Christian, who
Was nurse to me in childhood; such a nurse!—
You'd not believe!—who let me miss a mother
So little!—God requite it her!—But who   60
So frightened me as well! tormented so!
SITTAH. Concerning what? For what? and how?
RACHEL.   Poor Daya—
I told you—she's a Christian—and she must
Torment for love;—is one of those fanatics,
Who think they know the universal way,
The one true way to God!
SITTAH.   Oh, now I see!
RACHEL. And feel impelled to guide into that way
Each soul who's missed it.—Nor can they indeed
Do otherwise. For if it's true that this
Alone's the right way, how can they look on   70
With calmness as their friends go other ways,—
Which leads them to destruction everlasting?
It must be possible, the selfsame man
At once to love and hate.—Nor is it this
Which now at last compels me to complain
Aloud of her. Her sighing, warning, prayers,
Her threats I'd gladly longer yet endured;
At least that always led me into thoughts
Both good and useful. Who's not flattered, too,

At bottom, to be held of so much worth,   80
By whomsoever, that he can't endure
The thought of losing us for evermore.
SITTAH. Quite true!
RACHEL.   And yet—and yet—that goes too far!
For that I have no counter-weight; no patience,
Reflection; nothing!
SITTAH.   So? for what?
RACHEL.   For that
Which she insists just now she has disclosed.
SITTAH. Disclosed? just now?
RACHEL.   And only now! We neared,
As we were coming hither at your call,
A ruined Christian temple. Suddenly
She stopped; appeared to struggle with herself; and
    looked   90
Wet-eyed now at the sky, now me. "O come,"
At last she said, "let us the straight way take
Which through this temple leads." She goes; I
    follow,
My eyes astray with horror in the ruins
Unstable. Now again she stops; and I
Am with her at the sunken, rotten steps
Of some old altar. How I felt when she
With burning tears, with wringing hands, dropped
    down
Before my feet . . .
SITTAH.   Good child!
RACHEL.   And in the name
Of her who there had once heard many a prayer,
Performed so many a miracle, conjured me;—   101
With looks of true compassion, yes, conjured me
To have some pity on myself!—at least

To pardon her if she must now reveal
Her church's claim on me.

SITTAH *(aside).*   Unhappy girl!—
I sensed as much!

RACHEL.   I was of Christian blood;
Was baptized; was not Nathan's daughter, nor
Was he my father!—God! He not my father!—
O Sittah! See me at your feet anew!

SITTAH. No, don't! Get up! My brother comes! Get
up!   110

SCENE 7

SALADIN *(entering).* What's all this? Sittah?

SITTAH.   She's beside herself!

SALADIN. Who is it?

SITTAH.   Why, you know . . .

SALADIN.   Our Nathan's daughter?
What ails her?

SITTAH.   To your senses, child!—The Sultan . . .

RACHEL *(dragging herself on her knees to Saladin's
     feet, her head lowered to the floor).* I'll not get
     up! not sooner!—do not care
Sooner to see the Sultan's face!—admire
The glory of eternal justice shining
With goodness in his eyes, upon his brow . . .

SALADIN. Get up . . . get up!

RACHEL.   Until he promise me . . .

SALADIN. Come! I will promise . . . Be it what it will!

RACHEL. Not more nor less than leave to me my
     father;   10
And me to him!—I still don't know who else
Desires to be my father; or who can.

Nor would I know. Is blood then all that makes
The father? blood alone?

SALADIN *(lifting her up)*. I see, I see!—
Who was so cruel as to put such thoughts
Into your head? For is the fact established?
And proven?

RACHEL.   Must be! For my Daya claims
To have it from my wet-nurse.

SALADIN.   From your wet-nurse!

RACHEL. In dying she had felt herself obliged
To tell it her.   20

SALADIN.   Just dying?—And not drivelling
Already?—What if true!—Yes, blood alone
Is far from all that makes a father! scarce
Can make the father of a beast! at most
Confers the first right to acquire that name!—
Don't let yourself be frightened!—And you know
What I suggest? So soon as fathers twain
Are fighting for you:—quit them both: and take
A third one!—Take me then to be your father!

SITTAH. Do that, do that!

SALADIN.   I'll be to you a good,
A right good father!—Stop! I have a thought   30
Much   better   yet.—What   need   have   you   of
        fathers,
I'd like to know? Suppose they die? Let's look
Betimes for someone who would like to live
While keeping step with us! Know you of none? . . .

SITTAH. Don't make her blush!

SALADIN.   That's just what I had planned.
For blushing beautifies the ugly ones:
And should it not make lovely ones more lovely?—
I've bade your father, Nathan, and another—

One other hither. Can you guess him?—Hither!
You'll grant me your permission, Sittah?   40
SITTAH.   Brother!
SALADIN. At sight of him you must blush very much,
    Dear girl!
RACHEL.   At sight of whom? I, blush?
SALADIN.   Dissembler!
    Then blanch instead!—Do what you will and can!—
    (A slave-girl enters and approaches Sittah.)
    Could they be here already?
SITTAH *(to the slave)*.   Show them in.—
    It's they, my brother! *(Enter Nathan and Templar.)*

SCENE 8

SALADIN.   Ah, my good, dear friends!—
    First I must tell you, Nathan, that your gold
    You can have fetched again, so soon as you
    Desire it!
NATHAN.   Sultan! . . .
SALADIN.   Now I'm at your service
    In turn . . .
NATHAN.   Ah, Sultan!
SALADIN.   Now the caravan
    Is here. And once again I'm richer than
    I've been this long time.—Tell me what you need
    To undertake some major project! For
    You too, you too, you men of business, can
    Not have too much of cash!   10
NATHAN.   And why speak first
    Of such a trifle?—There I see an eye
    In tears, which I am far more willed to dry. *(Goes
    to Rachel.)*

You've wept? What ails you?—aren't you still my
    daughter?

RACHEL. My father! . . .

NATHAN.   Yes, we understand each other.
    Enough!—Be cheerful! Be composed! If but
    Your heart is still your own! If but no loss
    Can menace still your heart!—Your father is
    Not lost to you!

RACHEL.   No other, no!

TEMPLAR.   No other?—
    Then I've deceived myself. What one fears not
    To lose, one has not thought to own, and never   20
    Desired.—All's well, all's well!—That alters, Nathan,
    That alters all!—We came, O Saladin,
    At your command. But now it seems I had
    Misled you: so concern yourself no more.

SALADIN. Again so rash, young man!—Shall everything
    Conform to you? and all men guess your thoughts?

TEMPLAR. Well, don't you hear, and see it, Sultan?

SALADIN.   Truly,
    It's bad enough that you were not more sure
    Of your own case.

TEMPLAR.   I am so now.

SALADIN.   Whoever
    Presumes like that on any benefaction   30
    Would take it back. What you have rescued, is
    Not yours to own. Else were the robber, whom
    His greed lures into flames, a hero quite
    As good as you! *(Going to Rachel, to lead her to
    the Templar.)*
              Come, darling maiden, come!
    Don't judge him too severely. For if he
    Were otherwise; were not so warm and proud;

He never would have made attempt to save you.
Weigh one against the other.—Come! And shame
  him!
Do what he ought to do! Confess to him
Your love! Make offer of yourself to him!   40
And if he scorns you; if he should forget,
How in this act you do far more for him
Than he for you . . . What did he do for you?
Just smoked himself a bit!—is that so much?—
Then he has nothing of my brother Assad!
He only wears his mask, bears not his heart.
Come, dear . . .

SITTAH.   Now go, dear, go! It's still not much
  For all your gratitude; it's nothing yet.

NATHAN. Halt, Saladin! Halt, Sittah!

SALADIN.   What, you too?

NATHAN. One other has a voice here . . .   50

SALADIN.   Who denies it?—
  Indubitably, Nathan, there's a vote
  That's due a foster-father such as you!
  The first one, if you will.—You see I know
  All sides of the affair.

NATHAN.   No, no, not all!—
  I speak not of myself. There is another;
  A very different one, whom, Saladin,
  I beg you first to hear.

SALADIN.   Who?

NATHAN.   It's her brother!

SALADIN. What, Rachel's brother?

NATHAN.   Yes!

RACHEL.   My brother? Then
  I have a brother?

TEMPLAR (starting up from his sullen, silent inatten-

tion) . . Where? where is this brother?
Not yet at hand? I was to meet him here.   60
NATHAN. Be patient!
TEMPLAR *(in utmost bitterness).* He's palmed off a
     father on her:
How should he fail to find a brother too?
SALADIN. That caps the climax! Christian! Such a base
Suspicion had not crossed my Assad's lips.—
All right! keep on like that!
NATHAN.   Forgive him, do!—
I do so gladly.—Who can say what we
In his position, at his age, would think!
(Going to him in a friendly manner.)
Of course, sir Knight!—Distrust leads to sus-
     picion!—
If only you your *true* name had revealed
To me at once . . .   70
TEMPLAR.   What?
NATHAN.   You are not a Stauffen!
TEMPLAR. Who am I then?
NATHAN.   Your name's not Curt von Stauffen!
TEMPLAR. Then what's my name?
NATHAN.   It's Leu von Filnek.
TEMPLAR.   What?
NATHAN. You start?
TEMPLAR.   I should! Who says so?
NATHAN.   I; who can
Tell you much more. Yet charge you with no lie.
TEMPLAR. You don't?
NATHAN.   For it may be, that other name
Is yours by right as well.
TEMPLAR.   It is indeed!
(Aside.) God put that on his tongue!

NATHAN.   Yes, for your mother—
She was a Stauffen. And her brother, whom
Your parents asked in Germany to rear
Their child, when they, to flee that rugged climate,
Returned here to this land:—his name was Curt   81
Von Stauffen; possibly as his own child
Adopted you!—How long is it since you
Came hither with him? Is he still alive?

TEMPLAR. What shall I answer?—Nathan! To be sure!
You're right. But he is dead. I only came
With final reinforcements of our Order.—
But tell me—what has all this tale to do
With Rachel's brother?

NATHAN.   Now, your father . . .

TEMPLAR.   What
You knew him too? Him too?   90

NATHAN.   He was my friend.

TEMPLAR. He was your friend? How wonderful! . . .

NATHAN.   He called
Him Wolf von Filnek; but he was no German . . .

TEMPLAR. You know that too?

NATHAN.   Was only married to
A German; only briefly went with her
To Germany . . .

TEMPLAR.   Enough! I beg you, stop!—
But Rachel's brother? Rachel's brother . . .

NATHAN.   That
Is you!

TEMPLAR. I? I her brother?

RACHEL.   He my brother?

SITTAH. Brother and sister!

SALADIN.   Really! Is it true?

RACHEL *(going toward him).*   Ah! my brother!

TEMPLAR *(stepping backward)*. Her brother!

RACHEL *(stops and turns to Nathan)*.   It can-
    not be! His heart

    Knows nothing of it!—We're impostors! God!   100

SALADIN *(to the Templar)*. Impostors?—what? You
    think that? You can think it?

    Impostor, you! For everything's a lie

    In you: Your face and voice and walk! You're
    nothing!

    What, not acknowledge such a sister? Go!

TEMPLAR *(approaching him humbly)*. Do not you too
    misread my wonderment!

    Misjudge not in a moment, in the like

    Of which I think you never saw your Assad,

    Both him and me! *(Swiftly to Nathan.)*

                      You take and give me, Nathan!

    And both in full!—But no, you give me more

    Than you are taking! Infinitely more!   110

    (Throwing his arms about Rachel.)

    Oh, you my sister, darling sister!

NATHAN.   Blanda

    Von Filnek!

TEMPLAR.   Blanda, Blanda?—And not Rachel?

    No more your Rachel?—Heavens! You disown

    Your daughter, give her back her Christian name?

    Disown her for my sake!—O Nathan, Nathan!

    Why should she suffer? she!

NATHAN.   No thought of that!—

    O children mine, dear children!—For should not

    My daughter's brother be my child as well—

    Soon as he will? *(As he surrenders to their embraces,
        Saladin joins his sister in uneasy astonishment.)*

SALADIN. What say you to this, sister?

SITTAH. I'm greatly moved . . .   120

SALADIN.   And I—I'm shivering,
  Almost afraid of yet a greater shock!
  Prepare yourself for that as best you can.

SITTAH. What?

SALADIN.   Nathan, just a word with you! one word!—
  (As Nathan goes to him, Sittah joins the others to
    express her sympathy; Nathan and Saladin speak
    more softly.)
  Hark to me, Nathan! Said you not just now
  That—

NATHAN. What?

SALADIN.   Her father had from Germany
  Not come; was not a German born?
  What was he, then? Whence else could he have
    come?

NATHAN. That's something he would not reveal to me.
  And from his lips I know no word of it.

SALADIN. But he was not a Frank? no Westerner?   130

NATHAN. O, that he made no effort to conceal.—
  He spoke by preference Persian . . .

SALADIN.   Persian? Persian?
  What need I more?—It's he! Was he!

NATHAN.   What, who?

SALADIN. My brother! not a doubt! My Assad! not
  A doubt!

NATHAN.   Well, if you hit on that yourself:—
  Take the assurance in this volume here.
  (Hands him the breviary.)

SALADIN *(opening it eagerly)*. His writing! Ah! That
  too I'd know again!

NATHAN. As yet they do not know. It lies with you
  Alone, how much of it they shall be told!

SALADIN *(paging in the book)*. I not to recognize my
    brother's children?   [140]
  My niece and nephew—as I would my own?
  Not recognize them? I? And let you have them?
  (Aloud.)
  It's they. It's they, my Sittah! See, it's they!
  And both are my . . . that is, your brother's children!
  (He rushes to embrace them.)
SITTAH *(following him)*. What do I hear?—Could not
    be otherwise!
SALADIN *(to the Templar)*. And now, you spitfire,
    now you'll have to love me!
  (To Rachel.) And now I am what I proposed to be!
  Whether you will or no!
SITTAH.   I too, I too!
SALADIN *(back to the Templar)*. My son; my Assad!
  Yes, my Assad's son!
TEMPLAR. I of your blood!—So then those dreams of
    mine,   150
  With which they rocked me in my childhood,
    were—
  More than just dreams! *(Falling at his feet.)*
SALADIN *(raising him)*. Just see that scoundrel here!
  He knew some of the truth, and yet he could
  Consent to make me murder him! You wait!
  (Amid silent embraces on all sides the curtain falls.)